. . . YOU WILL NOT CATCH EITHER ONE.

RUSSIAN PROVERB

CONTENTS

1 THE ONE THING

> "Be like a postage stamp—stick to one thing until you get there."
>
> —Josh Billings

On June 7, 1991, the earth moved for 112 minutes. Not really, but it felt that way.

I was watching the hit comedy *City Slickers,* and the audience's laughter rattled and rocked the theater. Considered one of the funniest movies of all time, it also sprinkled in unexpected doses of wisdom and insight. In one memorable scene, Curly, the gritty cowboy played by the late Jack Palance, and city slicker Mitch, played by Billy Crystal, leave the group to search for stray cattle. Although they had clashed for most of the movie, riding along together they finally connect over a conversation about life. Suddenly, Curly reins his horse to a stop and turns in the saddle to face Mitch.

Curly: Do you know what the secret of life is?

Mitch: No. What?

Curly: This. [He holds up one finger.]

Mitch: Your finger?

Curly: One thing. Just one thing. You stick to that and everything else don't mean sh*t.

Mitch: That's great, but what's the "one thing"?

Curly: That's what you've got to figure out.

Out of the mouth of a fictional character to our ears comes the secret of success. Whether the writers knew it or unwittingly stumbled on it, what they wrote was the absolute truth. The ONE Thing is the best approach to getting what you want.

I didn't really get this until much later. I'd experienced success in the past, but it wasn't until I hit a wall that I began to connect my results with my approach. In less than a decade we'd built a successful company with national and international ambitions, but all of a sudden things weren't working out. For all the dedication and hard work, my life was in turmoil and it felt as if everything was crumbling around me.

I was failing.

SOMETHING HAD TO GIVE

At the end of a short rope that looked eerily like a noose, I sought help and found it in the form of a coach. I walked him through my situation and talked through the challenges I faced, both personal and professional. We revisited my goals and the trajectory I wanted for my life, and with a full grasp of the issues, he set out in search of answers. His research was thorough. When we got back together, he had my organizational chart—essentially a bird's-eye view of the entire company—up on the wall.

Our discussion started with a simple question: "Do you know what you need to do to turn things around?" I hadn't a clue.

He said there was only one thing I needed to do. He had identified 14 positions that needed new faces, and he believed that with the right individuals in those key spots, the company, my job, and my life would see a radical change for the better. I was shocked and let him know I thought it would take a lot more than that.

He said, "No. Jesus needed 12, but you'll need 14."

It was a transformational moment. I had never considered how so few could change so much. What became obvious is that, as focused as I thought I was, I wasn't focused enough. Finding 14 people was clearly the most important thing I could do. So, based on this meeting, I made a huge decision. I fired myself.

I stepped down as CEO and made finding those 14 people my singular focus.

This time the earth really did move. Within three years, we began a period of sustained growth that averaged 40 percent year-over-year for almost a decade. We grew from a regional player to an international contender. Extraordinary success showed up, and we never looked back.

As success begat success, something else happened along the way. The language of the ONE Thing emerged.

Having found the 14, I began working with our top people individually to build their careers and businesses. Out of habit, I would end our coaching calls with a recap of the handful of things they were agreeing to accomplish before our next session. Unfortunately, many would get most of them done, but not necessarily what mattered most. Results suffered. Frustration followed. So, in an effort to help them succeed, I started shortening my list: If you can do just three things this week. . . . If you can do just two things this week. . . . Finally, out of desperation, I went as small as I could possibly go and asked: *"What's the ONE Thing you can do this week such that by doing it everything else would be easier or unnecessary?"* And the most awesome thing happened.

Results went through the roof.

After these experiences, I looked back at my successes and failures and discovered an interesting pattern. Where I'd had huge success, I had narrowed my concentration to one thing, and where my success varied, my focus had too.

And the light came on.

GOING SMALL

If everyone has the same number of hours in a day, why do some people seem to get so much more done than others? How do they do more, achieve more, earn more, have more? If time is the currency of achievement, then why are some able to cash in their allotment for more chips than others? The answer is they make getting to the heart of things the heart of their approach. They go small.

When you want the absolute best chance to succeed at anything you want, your approach should always be the same. Go small.

"Going small" is ignoring all the things you could do and doing what you should do. It's recognizing that not all things matter equally and finding the things that matter most. It's a tighter way to connect what you do with what you want. It's realizing that extraordinary results are directly determined by how narrow you can make your focus.

The way to get the most out of your work and your life is to go as small as possible. Most people think just the opposite. They think big success is time consuming and complicated. As a result, their calendars and to-do lists become overloaded and overwhelming. Success starts to feel out of reach, so they settle for less. Unaware that big success comes when we do a few things well, they get lost trying to do too much and in the end accomplish too little. Over time they lower their expectations, abandon their dreams, and allow their life to get small. This is the wrong thing to make small.

You have only so much time and energy, so when you spread yourself out, you end up spread thin. You want your achievements to add up, but that actually takes subtraction, not addition. You need to be doing fewer things for more effect instead of doing more things with side effects. The problem with trying to do too much is that even if it works, adding more to your work and your life without cutting anything brings a lot of bad with it: missed deadlines, disappointing results, high stress, long hours, lost sleep, poor diet, no exercise, and missed moments with family and friends—all in the name of going after something that is easier to get than you might imagine.

Going small is a simple approach to extraordinary results, and it works. It works all the time, anywhere and on anything. Why? Because it has only one purpose—to ultimately get you to the point.

When you go as small as possible, you'll be staring at one thing. And that's the point.

2 THE DOMINO EFFECT

"Every great change starts like falling dominoes."

—B J Thornton

In Leeuwarden, The Netherlands, on Domino Day, November 13, 2009, Weijers Domino Productions coordinated the world record domino fall by lining up more than 4,491,863 dominoes in a dazzling display. In this instance, a single domino set in motion a domino fall that cumulatively unleashed more than 94,000 joules of energy, which is as much energy as it takes for an average-sized male to do 545 pushups.

Each standing domino represents a small amount of potential energy; the more you line up, the more potential energy you've accumulated. Line up enough and, with a simple flick, you can start a chain reaction of surprising power. And Weijers Domino Productions proved it. When one thing, the right thing, is set in motion, it can topple many things. And that's not all.

In 1983, Lorne Whitehead wrote in the *American Journal of Physics* that he'd discovered that domino falls could not only topple many things, they could also topple bigger things. He described how a single domino is capable of bringing down another domino that is actually 50 percent larger.

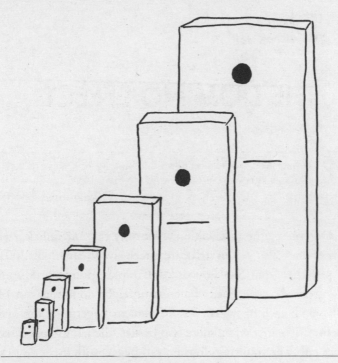

FIG. 1   A geometric domino progression.

DOMINOES –
A GEOMETRIC PROGRESSION

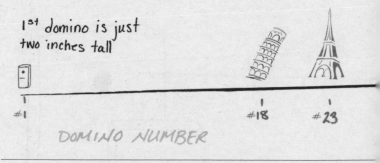

HEIGHT

1ˢᵗ domino is just two inches tall

#1   #18   #23

DOMINO NUMBER

FIG.2 A geometric progression is like a long, long train—it starts out too slow to notice until it's moving too fast to stop.

Do you see the implication? Not only can one knock over others but also others that are successively larger. In 2001 a physicist from San Francisco's Exploratorium reproduced Whitehead's experiment by creating eight dominoes out of plywood, each of which was 50 percent larger than the one before. The first was a mere two inches, the last almost three feet tall. The resulting domino fall began with a gentle tick and quickly ended "with a loud SLAM."

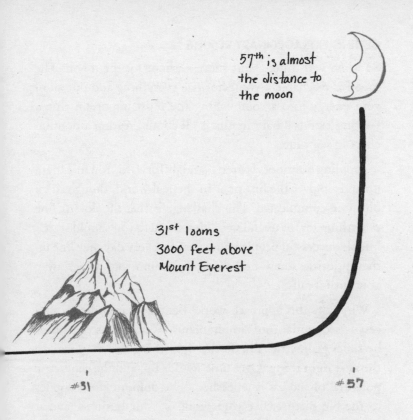

57th is almost the distance to the moon

31st looms 3000 feet above Mount Everest

#31

#57

Imagine what would happen if this kept going. If a regular domino fall is a *linear* progression, Whitehead's would be described as a *geometric* progression. The result could defy the imagination. The 10th domino would be almost as tall as NFL quarterback Peyton Manning. By the 18th, you're looking at a domino that would rival the Leaning Tower of Pisa. The 23rd domino would tower over the Eiffel Tower and the 31st domino would loom over Mount Everest by almost 3,000 feet. Number 57 would practically bridge the distance between the earth and the moon!

GETTING EXTRAORDINARY RESULTS

So when you think about success, shoot for the moon. The moon is reachable if you prioritize everything and put all of your energy into accomplishing the most important thing. Getting extraordinary results is all about creating a domino effect in your life.

Toppling dominoes is pretty straightforward. You line them up and tip over the first one. In the real world, though, it's a bit more complicated. The challenge is that life doesn't line everything up for us and say, "Here's where you should start." Highly successful people know this. So every day they line up their priorities anew, find the lead domino, and whack away at it until it falls.

Why does this approach work? Because extraordinary success is sequential, not simultaneous. What starts out linear becomes geometric. You do the right thing and then you do the next right thing. Over time it adds up, and the geometric potential of success is unleashed. The domino effect applies to the big picture, like your work or your business, and it applies to the smallest moment in each day when you're trying to decide what to do next. Success builds on success, and as this happens, over and over, you move toward the highest success possible.

When you see someone who has a lot of knowledge, they learned it over time. When you see someone who has a lot of skills, they developed them over time. When you see someone who has done a lot, they accomplished it over time. When you see someone who has a lot of money, they earned it over time.

The key is over time. Success is built sequentially. It's one thing at a time.

SUCCESS LEAVES CLUES **3**

Proof of the ONE Thing is everywhere. Look closely and you'll always find it.

> "It is those who concentrate on but one thing at a time who advance in this world."
>
> —Og Mandino

ONE PRODUCT, ONE SERVICE

Extraordinarily successful companies always have one product or service they're most known for or that makes them the most money. Colonel Sanders started KFC with a single secret chicken recipe. The Adolph Coors Company grew 1,500 percent from 1947 to 1967 with only one product, made in a single brewery. Microprocessors generate the vast majority of Intel's net revenue. And Starbucks? I think you know.

The list of businesses that have achieved extraordinary results through the power of the ONE Thing is endless. Sometimes what is made or delivered is also what is sold, sometimes not. Take Google. Their ONE Thing is search, which makes selling advertising, its key source of revenue, possible.

And what about *Star Wars*? Is the ONE Thing movies or merchandise? If you guessed merchandise, you'd be right—and you'd be wrong. Revenue from toys recently totaled over $10 billion, while combined worldwide box office revenue for the six main films totaled less than half that, $4.3 billion. From where I sit, movies are the ONE Thing because they make the toys and products possible.

The answer isn't always clear, but that doesn't make finding it any less important. Technological innovations, cultural shifts, and competitive forces will often dictate that a business's ONE Thing evolve or transform. The most successful companies know this and are always asking: "What's our ONE Thing?"

Apple is a study in creating an environment where an extraordinary ONE Thing can exist while transitioning to another extraordinary ONE Thing. From 1998 to 2012, Apple's ONE Thing moved from Macs to iMacs to iTunes to iPods to iPhones, with the iPad already jockeying for the pole position at the head of the product line. As each new "golden gadget" entered the limelight, the other products weren't discontinued or relegated to the discount tables. Those lines, plus others, continued to be refined while the current ONE Thing created a well-documented halo effect, making the user more likely to adopt the whole Apple product family.

When you get the ONE Thing, you begin to see the business world differently. If today your company doesn't know what its ONE Thing is, then the company's ONE Thing is to find out.

ONE PERSON

The ONE Thing is a dominant theme that shows up in different ways. Take the concept and apply it to people, and you'll see where one person makes all the difference. As a freshman in high school, Walt Disney took night courses at the Chicago Art Institute and became the cartoonist for his school newspaper. After graduation, he wanted to be a newspaper cartoonist but couldn't get a job, so his brother Roy, a businessman and banker, got him work at an art studio. It was there he learned animation and began creating animated cartoons. When Walt was young, his one person was Roy.

For Sam Walton, early on it was L. S. Robson, his father-in-law, who loaned him the $20,000 he needed to start his first retail business, a Ben Franklin franchise store. Then, when Sam was opening his first Wal-Mart, Robson secretly paid a landlord $20,000 to provide a pivotal expansion lease.

Albert Einstein had Max Talmud, his first mentor. It was Max who introduced a ten-year-old Einstein to key texts in math, science, and philosophy. Max took one meal a week with the Einstein family for six years while guiding young Albert.

No one is self-made.

> "There can only be one most important thing. Many things may be important, but only one can be the most important."
>
> —Ross Garber

Oprah Winfrey credits her father, and the time she spent with him and his wife, for "saving" her. She told Jill Nelson of *The Washington Post Magazine,* "If I hadn't been sent to my father, I would have gone in another direction." Professionally, it started with Jeffrey D. Jacobs, the "lawyer, agent, manager and financial adviser" who, when Oprah was looking for employment contract advice, persuaded her to establish her own company rather than simply be a talent for hire. Harpo Productions, Inc., was born.

The world is familiar with the influence that John Lennon and Paul McCartney had on each other's songwriting success, but in the recording studio there was George Martin. Considered one of the greatest record producers of all time, George has often been referred to as the "Fifth Beatle" for his extensive involvement on the Beatles' original albums. Martin's musical expertise helped fill the gaps between the Beatles' raw talent and the sound they wanted to achieve. Most of the Beatles' orchestral arrangements and instrumentation, as well as numerous keyboard parts on the early records, were written or performed by Martin in collaboration with the band.

Everyone has one person who either means the most to them or was the first to influence, train, or manage them.

No one succeeds alone. No one.

ONE PASSION, ONE SKILL

Look behind any story of extraordinary success and the ONE Thing is always there. It shows up in the life of any successful business and in the professional life of anyone successful. It also shows up around personal passions and skills. We each have passions and skills, but you'll see extraordinarily successful people with one intense emotion or one learned ability that shines through, defining them or driving them more than anything else.

Often, the line between passion and skill can be blurry. That's because they're almost always connected. Pat Matthews, one of America's great impressionist painters, says he turned his passion for painting into a skill, and ultimately a profession, by simply painting one painting a day. Angelo Amorico, Italy's most successful tour guide, says he developed his skills and ultimately his business from his singular passion for his country and the deep desire to share it with others. This is the story line for extraordinary success stories. Passion for something leads to disproportionate time practicing or working at it. That time spent eventually translates to skill, and when skill improves, results improve. Better results generally lead to more enjoyment, and more passion and more time is invested. It can be a virtuous cycle all the way to extraordinary results.

Gilbert Tuhabonye's one passion is running. Gilbert is an American long-distance runner born in Songa, Burundi, whose early love of track and field helped him win the Burundi National Championship in the men's 400 and 800 meters while only a junior in high school. This passion helped save his life.

On October 21, 1993, members of the Hutu tribe invaded Gilbert's high school and captured the students of the Tutsi tribe. Those not immediately killed were beaten and burned alive in a nearby building. After nine hours buried beneath burning bodies, Gilbert managed to escape and outrun his captors to the safety of a nearby hospital. He was the lone survivor.

> "You must be single-minded. Drive for the one thing on which you have decided."
>
> —General George S. Patton

He came to Texas and kept competing, honing his skills. Recruited by Abilene Christian University, Gilbert earned All-America honors six times. After graduation he moved to Austin, where by all accounts he is the most popular running coach in the city. To drill for water in Burundi, he cofounded the Gazelle Foundation, whose main fundraiser is—wait for it—"Run for the Water," a sponsored run through the streets of Austin. Do you see the theme running through his life?

From competitor to survivor, from college to career to charity, Gilbert Tuhabonye's passion for running became a skill that led to a profession that opened up an opportunity to give back. The smile he greets fellow runners with on the trails around Austin's Lady Bird Lake symbolizes how one passion can become one skill, and together ignite and define an extraordinary life.

The ONE Thing shows up time and again in the lives of the successful because it's a fundamental truth. It showed up for me, and if you let it, it will show up for you. Applying the ONE Thing to your work—and in your life—is the simplest and smartest thing you can do to propel yourself toward the success you want.

ONE LIFE

If I had to choose only one example of someone who has harnessed the ONE Thing to build an extraordinary life, it would be American businessman Bill Gates. Bill's one passion in high school was computers, which led him to develop one skill, computer programming. While in high school he met one person, Paul Allen, who gave him his first job and became his partner in forming Microsoft. This happened as the result of one letter they sent to one person, Ed Roberts, who changed their lives forever by giving them a shot at writing the code for one computer, the Altair 8800—and they needed only one shot. Microsoft began its life to do one thing, develop and sell BASIC interpreters for the Altair 8800, which eventually made Bill Gates the richest man in the world for 15 straight years. When he retired from Microsoft, Bill chose one person to replace him as CEO— Steve Ballmer, whom he met in college. By the way, Steve was Microsoft's 30th employee but the first business manager hired by Bill. And the story doesn't end there.

Bill and Melinda Gates decided to put their wealth to work making a difference in the world. Guided by the belief that every life has equal value, they formed one foundation to do ONE Thing: to tackle "really tough problems" like health and education. Since its inception, the majority of the foundation's grants have gone to one area, Bill and Melinda's Global Health Program. This ambitious program's one goal is to harness advances in science and technology to save lives in poor countries. To do this they eventually settled on one thing— stamp out infectious disease as a major cause of death in their lifetime. At some point in their journey, they made a decision to focus on one thing that would do this—vaccines. Bill explained the decision by saying, "We had to choose what the most impactful thing to give would be. . . . The magic tool of health intervention is vaccines, because they can be made inexpensively." A singular line of questioning led them down this one path when Melinda asked, "Where's the place you can have the biggest impact with the money?" Bill and Melinda Gates are living proof of the power of the ONE Thing.

ONE THING

The doors to the world have been flung wide open, and the view that's available is staggering. Through technology and innovation, opportunities abound and possibilities seem endless. As inspiring as this can be, it can be equally overwhelming. The unintended consequence of abundance is that we are bombarded with more information and choices in a day than our ancestors received in a lifetime. Harried and hurried, a nagging sense that we attempt too much and accomplish too little haunts our days.

We sense intuitively that the path to more is through less, but the question is, Where to begin? From all that life has to offer, how do you choose? How do you make the best decisions possible, experience life at an extraordinary level, and never look back?

Live the ONE Thing.

What Curly knew, all successful people know. The ONE Thing sits at the heart of success and is the starting point for achieving extraordinary results. Based on research and real-life experience, it's a big idea about success wrapped in a disarmingly simple package. Explaining it is easy; buying into it can be tough.

So, before we can have a frank, heart-to-heart discussion about how the ONE Thing actually works, I want to openly discuss the myths and misinformation that keep us from accepting it. They are the lies of success.

Once we banish these from our minds, we can take up the ONE Thing with an open mind and a clear path.

THE LIES
THEY MISLEAD AND DERAIL US

> "It ain't what you don't know that gets you into trouble. It's what you know for sure that just ain't so."
>
> —*Mark Twain*

THE TROUBLE WITH "TRUTHINESS"

In 2003, Merriam-Webster began analyzing searches on their online dictionary to determine the "Word of the Year." The idea was that since online searches for words reveal whatever is on our collective minds, then the most searched-for word should capture the spirit of the times. The debut winner delivered. On the heels of the invasion of Iraq, it seems everyone wanted to know what "democracy" really meant. The next year, "blog," a little made-up word that described a new way to communicate, topped the list. After all the political scandals of 2005, "integrity" earned top honors.

Then, in 2006, Merriam-Webster added a twist. Site visitors could nominate candidates and subsequently vote on the "Word of the Year." You could say it was an effort to instill a quantitative exercise with qualitative feedback, or you could just call it good marketing. The winner, by a five-to-one landslide, was "truthiness," a word comedian Stephen Colbert coined as "truth that comes from the gut, not books" on the debut episode of his Comedy Central show, *The Colbert Report*. In an Information Age driven by round-the-clock news, ranting talk radio, and editorless blogging, truthiness captures all the incidental, accidental, and even intentional falsehoods that sound just "truthy" enough for us to accept as true.

The problem is we tend to act on what we believe even when what we believe isn't anything we should. As a result, buying into The ONE Thing becomes difficult because we've unfortunately bought into too many others—and more often than not those "other things" muddle our thinking, misguide our actions, and sidetrack our success.

Life is too short to chase unicorns. It's too precious to rely on a rabbit's foot. The real solutions we seek are almost always hiding in plain sight; unfortunately, they've usually been obscured by an unbelievable amount of bunk, an astounding flood of "common sense" that turns out to be nonsense. Ever hear your boss evoke the frog-in-boiling-water metaphor? ("Toss a frog into a pot of hot water and it will jump right back out. But if you place a frog in lukewarm water and slowly raise the temperature, it will boil to death.") It's a lie—a very truthy lie, but a lie nonetheless. Anyone ever tell you "fish stink from the head down"? Not true. Just a fish tale that actually turns out to be fishy. Ever hear about how the explorer Cortez burned his ships on arriving at the Americas to motivate his men? Not true. Another lie. "Bet on the jockey, not the horse!" has long been a rallying cry for placing your faith in a company's leadership. However, as a betting strategy, this maxim will put you on the fast track to the pauper's house, which makes you wonder how it ever became a maxim at all. Over time, myths and mistruths get thrown around so often they eventually feel familiar and start to sound like the truth.

Then we start basing important decisions on them.

The challenge we all face when forming our success strategies is that, just like tales of frogs, fish, explorers, and jockeys, success has its own lies too. "I just have too much that has to be done." "I'll get more done by doing things at the same time." "I need to be a more disciplined person." "I should be able to do what I want whenever I want." "I need more balance in my life." "Maybe I shouldn't dream so big." Repeat these thoughts often enough and they become the six lies about success that keep us from living The ONE Thing.

THE SIX LIES BETWEEN YOU AND SUCCESS

1. Everything Matters Equally

2. Multitasking

3. A Disciplined Life

4. Willpower Is Always on Will-Call

5. A Balanced Life

6. Big Is Bad

The six lies are beliefs that get into our heads and become operational principles driving us the wrong way. Highways that end as bunny trails. Fool's gold that diverts us from the mother lode. If we're going to maximize our potential, we're going to have to make sure we put these lies to bed.

4 EVERYTHING MATTERS EQUALLY

"Things which matter most must never be at the mercy of things which matter least."

—Johann Wolfgang von Goethe

Equality is a worthy ideal pursued in the name of justice and human rights. In the real world of results, however, things are never equal. No matter how teachers grade—two students are not equal. No matter how fair officials try to be—contests are not equal. No matter how talented people are—no two are ever equal. A dime equals ten cents and people must absolutely be treated fairly, but in the world of achievement everything doesn't matter equally.

Equality is a lie.

Understanding this is the basis of all great decisions.

So, how do you decide? When you have a lot to get done in the day, how do you decide what to do first? As kids, we mostly did things we needed to do when it was time to do them. *It's breakfast time. It's time to go to school, time to do homework, time to do chores, bath time, bedtime.* Then, as we got older, we were given a measure of discretion. *You can go out and play as long as you get your homework done before dinner.* Later, as we became adults, everything became discretionary. It all became our choice. And when our lives are defined by our choices, the all-important question becomes, How do we make good ones?

Complicating matters, the older we get, it seems there is more and more piled on that we believe "simply must get done." Overbooked, overextended, and overcommitted. "In the weeds" overwhelmingly becomes our collective condition.

That's when the battle for the right of way gets fierce and frantic. Lacking a clear formula for making decisions, we get reactive and fall back on familiar, comfortable ways to decide what to do. As a result, we haphazardly select approaches that undermine our success. Pinballing through our day like a confused character in a B-horror movie, we end up running up the stairs instead of out the front door. The best decision gets traded for any decision, and what should be progress simply becomes a trap.

When everything feels urgent and important, everything seems equal. We become active and busy, but this doesn't actually move us any closer to success. Activity is often unrelated to productivity, and busyness rarely takes care of business.

> "The things which are most important don't always scream the loudest."
>
> —Bob Hawke

As Henry David Thoreau said, "It's not enough to be busy, so are the ants. The question is, what are we busy about?" Knocking out a hundred tasks for whatever the reason is a poor substitute for doing even one task that's meaningful. Not everything matters equally, and success isn't a game won by whoever does the most. Yet that is exactly how most play it on a daily basis.

MUCH TO-DO ABOUT NOTHING

To-do lists are a staple of the time-management-and-success industry. With our wants and others' wishes flying at us right and left, we impulsively jot them down on scraps of paper in moments of clarity or build them methodically on printed notepads. Time planners reserve valuable space for daily, weekly, and monthly task lists. Apps abound for taking to-dos mobile, and software programs code them right into their menus. It seems that everywhere we turn we're encouraged to make lists—and though lists are invaluable, they have a dark side.

While to-dos serve as a useful collection of our best intentions, they also tyrannize us with trivial, unimportant stuff that we feel obligated to get done—because it's on our list. Which is why most of us have a love-hate relationship with our to-dos. If allowed, they set our priorities the same way an inbox can dictate our day. Most inboxes overflow with unimportant e-mails masquerading as priorities. Tackling these tasks in the order we receive them is behaving as if the squeaky wheel immediately deserves the grease. But, as Australian prime minister Bob Hawke duly noted, "The things which are most important don't always scream the loudest."

Achievers operate differently. They have an eye for the essential. They pause just long enough to decide what matters and then allow what matters to drive their day. Achievers do sooner what others plan to do later and defer, perhaps indefinitely, what others do sooner. The difference isn't in intent, but in right of way. Achievers always work from a clear sense of priority.

Left in its raw state, as a simple inventory, a to-do list can easily lead you astray. A to-do list is simply the things you think you need to do; the first thing on your list is just the first thing you thought of. To-do lists inherently lack the intent of success. In fact, most to-do lists are actually just survival lists—getting you through your day and your life, but not making each day a stepping-stone for the next so that you sequentially build a successful life. Long hours spent checking off a to-do list and ending the day with a full trash can and a clean desk are not virtuous and have nothing to do with success. Instead of a to-do list, you need a success list—a list that is purposefully created around extraordinary results.

To-do lists tend to be long; success lists are short. One pulls you in all directions; the other aims you in a specific direction. One is a disorganized directory and the other is an organized directive. If a list isn't built around success, then that's not where it takes you. If your to-do list contains everything, then it's probably taking you everywhere but where you really want to go.

So how does a successful person turn a to-do list into a success list? With so many things you *could* do, how do you decide what matters most at any given moment on any given day?

Just follow Juran's lead.

JURAN CRACKS THE CODE

In the late '30s a group of managers at General Motors made an intriguing discovery that opened the door for an amazing breakthrough. One of their card readers (input devices for early computers) started producing gibberish. While investigating the faulty machine, they stumbled on a way to encode secret messages. This was a big deal at the time. Since Germany's infamous Enigma coding machines first appeared in World War I, both code making and code breaking were the stuff of high national security and even higher public curiosity. The GM managers quickly became convinced that their accidental cipher was unbreakable. One man, a visiting Western Electric consultant, disagreed. He took up the code-breaking challenge, worked into the night, and cracked the code by three o'clock the following morning. His name was Joseph M. Juran.

Juran later cited this incident as the starting point for cracking an even bigger code and making one of his greatest contributions to science and business. As a result of his deciphering success, a GM executive invited him to review research on management compensation that followed a formula described by a little-known Italian economist, Vilfredo Pareto. In the 19th century, Pareto had written a mathematical model for income distribution in Italy that stated that 80 percent of the land was owned by 20 percent of the people. Wealth was not evenly distributed. In fact, according to Pareto, it was actually concentrated in a highly predictable way. A pioneer of quality-control management, Juran had noticed that a handful of flaws would usually produce a majority of the defects. This imbalance not only rang true to his experience, but he suspected it might even be a universal law—and that what Pareto had observed might be bigger than even Pareto had imagined.

While writing his seminal book *Quality Control Handbook,* Juran wanted to give a short name to the concept of the "vital few and trivial many." One of the many illustrations in his manuscript was labeled "Pareto's principle of unequal distribution. . . ." Where another might have called it Juran's Rule, he called it Pareto's Principle.

Pareto's Principle, it turns out, is as real as the law of gravity, and yet most people fail to see the gravity of it. It's not just a theory—it is a provable, predictable certainty of nature and one of the greatest productivity truths ever discovered. Richard Koch, in his book *The 80/20 Principle,* defined it about as well as anyone: "The 80/20 Principle asserts that a minority of causes, inputs, or effort usually lead to a majority of the results, outputs, or rewards." In other words, in the world of success, things aren't equal. A small amount of causes creates most of the results. Just the right input creates most of the output. Selected effort creates almost all of the rewards.

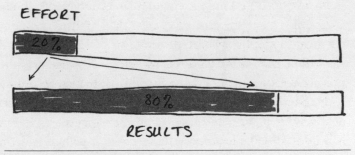

EFFORT

20%

80%

RESULTS

FIG. 3 The 80/20 Principle says the minority of your effort leads to the majority of your results.

Pareto points us in a very clear direction: the majority of what you want will come from the minority of what you do. Extraordinary results are disproportionately created by fewer actions than most realize.

Don't get hung up on the numbers. Pareto's truth is about inequality, and though often stated as an 80/20 ratio, it can actually take a variety of proportions. Depending on the circumstances, it can easily play out as, say, 90/20, where 90 percent of your success comes from 20 percent of your effort. Or 70/10 or 65/5. But understand that these are all fundamentally working off the same principle. Juran's great insight was that not everything matters equally; some things matter more than others—a lot more. A to-do list becomes a success list when you apply Pareto's Principle to it.

The 80/20 Principle has been one of the most important guiding success rules in my career. It describes the

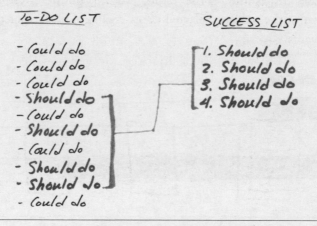

TO-DO LIST

- Could do
- Could do
- Could do
- Should do
- Could do
- Should do
- Could do
- Should do
- Should do
- Could do

SUCCESS LIST

1. Should do
2. Should do
3. Should do
4. Should do

FIG. 4   A to-do list becomes a success list when you prioritize it.

phenomenon which, like Juran, I've observed in my own life over and over again. A few ideas gave me most of my results. Some clients were far more valuable than others; a small number of people created most of my business success; and a handful of investments put the most money in my pocket. Everywhere I turned, the concept of unequal distribution popped up. The more it showed up, the more I paid attention—and the more I paid attention, the more it showed up. Finally I quit thinking it was a coincidence and began to apply it as the absolute principle of success that it is—not only to my life, but also in working with everyone else, as well. And the results were extraordinary.

EXTREME PARETO

Pareto proves everything I'm telling you—but there's a catch. He doesn't go far enough. I want you to go further. I want you to take Pareto's Principle to an extreme. I want you to go small by identifying the 20 percent, and then I want you to go even smaller by finding the vital few of the vital few. The 80/20 rule is the first word, but not the last, about success. What Pareto started, you've got to finish. Success requires that you follow the 80/20 Principle, but you don't have to stop there.

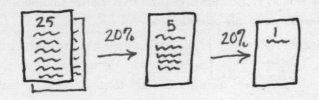

FIG. 5   No matter how many to-dos you start with, you can always narrow it to one.

Keep going. You can actually take 20 percent of the 20 percent of the 20 percent and continue until you get to the single most important thing! (See figure 5.) No matter the task, mission, or goal. Big or small. Start with as large a list as you want, but develop the mindset that you will whittle your way from there to the critical few and not stop until you end with the essential ONE. The imperative ONE. The ONE Thing.

In 2001, I called a meeting of our key executive team. As fast as we were growing, we were still not acknowledged by the very top people in our industry. I challenged our group to brainstorm 100 ways to turn this situation around. It took us all day to come up with the list. The next morning, we narrowed the list down to ten ideas, and from there we chose just one big idea. The one that we decided on was that I would write a book on how to become an elite performer in our industry. It worked. Eight years later that one book had not only become a national bestseller, but also had morphed into a series of books with total sales of over a million copies. In an industry of about a million people, one thing changed our image forever.

Now, again, stop and do the math. One idea out of 100. That is Pareto to the extreme. That's thinking big, but going very small. That's applying the ONE Thing to a business challenge in a truly powerful way.

But this doesn't just apply to business. On my 40th birthday, I started taking guitar lessons and quickly discovered I could give only 20 minutes a day to practice. This wasn't much, so I knew I had to narrow down what I learned. I asked my friend Eric Johnson (one of the greatest guitarists ever) for advice. Eric said that if I could do only one thing, then I should practice my scales. So, I took his advice and chose the minor blues scale. What I discovered was that if I learned that scale, then I could play many of the solos of great classic rock guitarists from Eric Clapton to Billy Gibbons and, maybe someday, even Eric Johnson. That scale became my ONE Thing for the guitar, and it unlocked the world of rock 'n' roll for me.

The inequality of effort for results is everywhere in your life if you will simply look for it. And if you apply this principle, it will unlock the success you seek in anything that matters to you. There will always be just a few things that matter more than the rest, and out of those, one will matter most. Internalizing this concept is like being handed a magic compass. Whenever you feel lost or lacking direction, you can pull it out to remind yourself to discover what matters most.

BIG IDEAS

1. **Go small.** Don't focus on being busy; focus on being productive. Allow what matters most to drive your day.

2. **Go extreme.** Once you've figured out what actually matters, keep asking what matters most until there is only one thing left. That core activity goes at the top of your success list.

3. **Say no.** Whether you say "later" or "never," the point is to say "not now" to anything else you could do until your most important work is done.

4. **Don't get trapped in the "check off" game.** If we believe things don't matter equally, we must act accordingly.

We can't fall prey to the notion that everything has to be done, that checking things off our list is what success is all about. We can't be trapped in a game of "check off" that never produces a winner. The truth is that things don't matter equally and success is found in doing what matters most.

Sometimes it's the first thing you do. Sometimes it's the only thing you do. Regardless, doing the most important thing is always the most important thing.

MULTITASKING 5

So, if doing the most important thing is the most important thing, why would you try to do anything else at the same time? It's a great question.

In the summer of 2009, Clifford Nass set out to answer just that. His mission? To find out how well so-called multitaskers multitasked. Nass, a professor at Stanford University, told the *New York Times* that he had been "in awe" of multitaskers and deemed himself to be a poor one. So he and his team of researchers gave 262

> "To do two things at once is to do neither."
>
> —*Publilius Syrus*

students questionnaires to determine how often they multi-tasked. They divided their test subjects into two groups of high and low multitaskers and began with the presumption that the frequent multitaskers would perform better. They were wrong.

"I was sure they had some secret ability," said Nass. "But it turns out that high multitaskers are suckers for irrelevancy." They were outperformed on every measure. Although they'd convinced themselves and the world that they were great at it, there was just one problem. To quote Nass, "Multitaskers were just lousy at everything."

Multitasking is a lie.

It's a lie because nearly everyone accepts it as an effective thing to do. It's become so mainstream that people actually think it's something they should do, and do as often as possible. We not only hear talk about doing it, we even hear talk about getting better at it. More than six million webpages offer answers on how to do it, and career websites list "multitasking" as a skill for employers to target and for prospective hires to list as a strength. Some have gone so far as to be proud of their supposed skill and have adopted it as a way of life. But it's actually a "way of lie," for the truth is multitasking is neither efficient nor effective. In the world of results, it will fail you every time.

> "Multitasking is merely the opportunity to screw up more than one thing at a time."
>
> —Steve Uzzell

When you try to do two things at once, you either can't or won't do either well. If you think multitasking is an effective way to get more done, you've got it backward. It's an effective way to get less done. As Steve Uzzell said, "Multitasking is merely the opportunity to screw up more than one thing at a time."

MONKEY MIND

The concept of humans doing more than one thing at a time has been studied by psychologists since the 1920s, but the term "multitasking" didn't arrive on the scene until the 1960s. It was used to describe computers, not people. Back then, ten megahertz was apparently so mind-bogglingly fast that a whole new word was needed to describe a computer's ability to quickly perform many tasks. In retrospect, they probably made a poor choice, for the expression "multitasking" is inherently deceptive. Multitasking is about multiple tasks *alternately* sharing one resource (the CPU), but in time the context was flipped and it became interpreted to mean multiple tasks being done *simultaneously* by one resource (a person). It was a clever turn of phrase that's misleading, for even computers can process only one piece of code at a time. When they "multitask," they switch back and forth, alternating their attention until both tasks are done. The speed with which computers tackle multiple tasks feeds the illusion that everything happens at the same time, so comparing computers to humans can be confusing.

People can actually do two or more things at once, such as walk and talk, or chew gum and read a map; but, like computers, what we can't do is focus on two things at once. Our attention bounces back and forth. This is fine for computers, but it has serious repercussions in humans. Two airliners are cleared to land on the same runway. A patient is given the wrong medicine. A toddler is left unattended in the bathtub. What all these potential tragedies share is that people are trying to do too many things at once and forget to do something they should do.

It's strange, but somehow over time the image of the modern human has become one of a multitasker. We think we can, so we think we should. Kids studying while texting, listening to music, or watching television. Adults driving while talking on the phone, eating, applying makeup, or even shaving. Doing something in one room while talking to someone in the next. Smartphones in hands before napkins hit laps. It's not that we have too little time to do all the things we need to do, it's that we feel the need to do too many things in the time we have. So we double and triple up in the hope of getting everything done.

And then there's work.

The modern office is a carnival of distracting multitasking demands. While you diligently try to complete a project, someone has a coughing fit in a nearby cubicle and asks if you have a lozenge. The office paging system continually calls out messages that anyone within earshot of an intercom hears. You're alerted around the clock to new e-mails arriving in your inbox while your social media newsfeed keeps trying to catch your eye and your cell phone intermittently vibrates on the desk to the tune of a new text. A stack of unopened mail and piles of unfinished work sit within sight as people keep swinging by your desk all day to ask you questions. Distraction, disturbance, disruption. Staying on task is exhausting. Researchers estimate that workers are interrupted every 11 minutes and then spend almost a third of their day recovering from these distractions. And yet amid all of this we still assume we can rise above it and do what has to be done within our deadlines.

But we're fooling ourselves. Multitasking is a scam. Poet laureate Billy Collins summed it up well: "We call it multitasking, which makes it sound like an ability to do lots of things at the same time. . . . A Buddhist would call this monkey mind." We think we're mastering multitasking, but we're just driving ourselves bananas.

JUGGLING IS AN ILLUSION

We come by it naturally. With an average of 4,000 thoughts a day flying in and out of our heads, it's easy to see why we try to multitask. If a change in thought every 14 seconds is an invitation to change direction, then it's rather obvious we're continually tempted to try to do too much at once. While doing one thing we're only seconds away from thinking of something else we could do. Moreover, history suggests that our continued existence may have required that human beings evolve to be able to oversee multiple tasks at the same time. Our ancestors wouldn't have lasted long if they couldn't scan for predators while gathering berries, tanning hides, or just idling by the fire after a hard day hunting. The pull to juggle more than one task at a time is not only at the core of how we're wired, but was most likely a necessity for survival.

But juggling isn't multitasking.

Juggling is an illusion. To the casual observer, a juggler is juggling three balls at once. In reality, the balls are being independently caught and thrown in rapid succession. Catch, toss, catch, toss, catch, toss. One ball at a time. It's what researchers refer to as "task switching."

When you switch from one task to another, voluntarily or not, two things happen. The first is nearly instantaneous: you decide to switch. The second is less predictable: you have to activate the "rules" for whatever you're about to do (see figure 6). Switching between two simple tasks—like watching television and folding clothes—is quick and relatively painless. However, if you're working on a spreadsheet and a co-worker

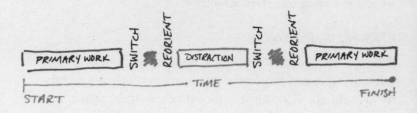

INTERRUPTED WORKFLOW

| PRIMARY WORK | SWITCH | REORIENT | DISTRACTION | SWITCH | REORIENT | PRIMARY WORK |

TIME

START ——————————————————————————— FINISH

FOCUSED WORKFLOW

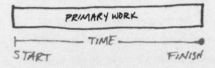

| PRIMARY WORK |

TIME

START ——————— FINISH

FIG 6 Multitasking doesn't save time—it wastes time.

pops into your office to discuss a business problem, the relative complexity of those tasks makes it impossible to easily jump back and forth. It always takes some time to start a new task and restart the one you quit, and there's no guarantee that you'll ever pick up exactly where you left off. There is a price for this. "The cost in terms of extra time from having to task switch depends on how complex or simple the tasks are," reports researcher Dr. David Meyer. "It can range from time increases of 25 percent or less for simple tasks to well over 100 percent or more for very complicated tasks." Task switching exacts a cost few realize they're even paying.

BRAIN CHANNELS

So, what's happening when we're actually doing two things at once? It's simple. We've separated them. Our brain has channels, and as a result we're able to process different kinds of data in different parts of our brain. This is why you can talk and walk at the same time. There is no channel interference. But here's the catch: you're not really focused on both activities. One is happening in the foreground and the other in the background. If you were trying to talk a passenger through landing a DC-10, you'd stop walking. Likewise, if you were walking across a gorge on a rope bridge, you'd likely stop talking. You can do two things at once, but you can't focus effectively on two things at once. Even my dog Max knows this. When I get caught up with a basketball game on TV, he gives me a good nudge. Apparently, background scratches can be pretty unsatisfying.

Many think that because their body is functioning without their conscious direction, they're multitasking. This is true, but not the way they mean it. A lot of our physical actions, like breathing, are being directed from a different part of our brain than where focus comes from. As a result, there's no channel conflict. We're right when we say something is "front and center" or "top of mind," because that's where focus occurs—in the prefrontal cortex. When you focus, it's like shining a spotlight on what matters. You can actually give attention to two things, but that is what's called "divided attention." And make no mistake. Take on two things and your attention gets divided. Take on a third and something gets dropped.

The problem of trying to focus on two things at once shows up when one task demands more attention or if it cross s into a channel already in use. When your spouse is descr -ing the way the living room furniture has been rearran d, you engage your visual cortex to see it in your mind's ye. If you happen to be driving at that moment, this channel interference means you are now seeing the new sofa and love seat combination and are effectively blind to the car braking in front of you. You simply can't effectively focus on two important things at the same time.

Every time we try to do two or more things at once, we're simply dividing up our focus and dumbing down all of the outcomes in the process. Here's the short list of how multitasking short-circuits us:

1. There is just so much brain capability at any one time. Divide it up as much as you want, but you'll pay a price in time and effectiveness.

2. The more time you spend switched to another task, the less likely you are to get back to your original task. This is how loose ends pile up.

3. Bounce between one activity and another and you lose time as your brain reorients to the new task. Those milliseconds add up. Researchers estimate we lose 28 percent of an average workday to multitasking ineffectiveness.

4. Chronic multitaskers develop a distorted sense of how long it takes to do things. They almost always believe tasks take longer to complete than is actually required.

5. Multitaskers make more mistakes than non-multitaskers. They often make poorer decisions because they favor new information over old, even if the older information is more valuable.

6. Multitaskers experience more life-reducing, happiness-squelching stress.

With research overwhelmingly clear, it seems insane that—knowing how multitasking leads to mistakes, poor choices, and stress—we attempt it anyway. Maybe it's just too tempting. Workers who use computers during the day change windows or check e-mail or other programs nearly 37 times an hour. Being in a distractible setting sets us up to be more distractible. Or maybe it's the high. Media multi-taskers actually experience a thrill with switching—a burst of dopamine—that can be addictive. Without it, they can feel bored. For whatever the reason, the results are unambiguous: multitasking slows us down and makes us slower witted.

DRIVEN TO DISTRACTION

In 2009, *New York Times* reporter Matt Richtel earned a Pulitzer Prize for National Reporting with a series of articles ("Driven to Distraction") on the dangers of driving while texting or using cell phones. He found that distracted driving is responsible for 16 percent of all traffic fatalities and nearly half a million injuries annually. Even an idle phone conversation when driving takes a 40 percent bite out of your focus and, surprisingly, can have the same effect as being drunk. The evidence is so compelling that many states and munici-palities have outlawed cell phone use while driving. This makes sense. Though some of us at times have been guilty, we'd never condone it for our teenage kids. All it takes is a text message to turn the family SUV into a deadly, two-ton battering ram. Multitasking can cause more than one type of wreck.

We know that multitasking can even be fatal when lives are at stake. In fact, we fully expect pilots and surgeons to focus on their jobs to the exclusion of everything else. And we expect that anyone in their position who gets caught doing otherwise will always be taken severely to task. We accept no arguments and have no tolerance for anything but total concentration from these professionals. And yet, here the rest of us are—living another standard. Do we not value our own job or take it as seriously? Why would we ever tolerate multi-tasking when we're doing our most important work? Just because our day job doesn't involve bypass surgery shouldn't make focus any less critical to our success or the success of others. Your work deserves no less respect. It may not seem so in the moment, but the connectivity of everything we do ultimately means that we each not only have a job to do, but a job that deserves to be done well. Think of it this way. If we really lose almost a third of our workday to distractions, what is the cumulative loss over a career? What is the loss to other careers? To businesses? When you think about it, you might just discover that if you don't figure out a way to resolve this, you could in fact lose your career or your business. Or worse, cause others to lose theirs.

On top of work, what sort of toll do our distractions take on our personal lives? Author Dave Crenshaw put it just right when he wrote, "The people we live with and work with on a daily basis deserve our full attention. When we give people segmented attention, piecemeal time, switching back and forth, the switching cost is higher than just the time involved. We end up damaging relationships." Every time I see a couple dining with one partner trying earnestly to communicate while the other is texting under the table, I'm reminded of the simple truth of that statement.

BIG IDEAS

1. **Distraction is natural.** Don't feel bad when you get distracted. Everyone gets distracted.

2. **Multitasking takes a toll.** At home or at work, distractions lead to poor choices, painful mistakes, and unnecessary stress.

3. **Distraction undermines results.** When you try to do too much at once, you can end up doing nothing well. Figure out what matters most in the moment and give it your undivided attention.

In order to be able to put the principle of The ONE Thing to work, you can't buy into the lie that trying to do two things at once is a good idea. Though multitasking is sometimes possible, it's never possible to do it effectively.

6 A DISCIPLINED LIFE

"It's one of the most prevalent myths of our culture: self-discipline."

—Leo Babauta

There is this pervasive idea that the successful person is the "disciplined person" who leads a "disciplined life."

It's a lie.

The truth is we don't need any more discipline than we already have. We just need to direct and manage it a little better.

Contrary to what most people believe, success is not a marathon of disciplined action. Achievement doesn't require you to be a full-time disciplined person where your every action is trained and where control is the solution to every situation. Success is actually a short race—a sprint fueled by discipline just long enough for habit to kick in and take over.

When we know something that needs to be done but isn't currently getting done, we often say, "I just need more discipline." Actually, we need the habit of doing it. And we need just enough discipline to build the habit.

In any discussion about success, the words "discipline" and "habit" ultimately intersect. Though separate in meaning, they powerfully connect to form the foundation for achievement—regularly working at something until it regularly works for you. When you discipline yourself, you're essentially training yourself to act in a specific way. Stay with this long enough and it becomes routine—in other words, a habit. So when you see people who look like "disciplined" people, what you're really seeing is people who've trained a handful of habits into their lives. This makes them seem "disciplined" when actually they're not. No one is.

And who would want to be, anyway? The very thought of having your every behavior molded and maintained by training seems frighteningly impossible on one hand and utterly boring on the other. Most people ultimately reach this conclusion but, seeing no alternative, redouble their efforts at the impossible or quietly quit. Frustration shows up and resignation eventually sets in.

You don't need to be a disciplined person to be successful. In fact, you can become successful with less discipline than you think, for one simple reason: success is about doing the right thing, not about doing everything right.

The trick to success is to choose the right habit and bring just enough discipline to establish it. That's it. That's all the discipline you need. As this habit becomes part of your life, you'll start looking like a disciplined person, but you won't be one. What you will be is someone who has something regularly working for you because you regularly worked on it. You'll be a person who used selected discipline to build a powerful habit.

SELECTED DISCIPLINE WORKS SWIMMINGLY

Olympic swimmer Michael Phelps is a case study of selected discipline. When he was diagnosed with ADHD as a child, his kindergarten teacher told his mother, "Michael can't sit still. Michael can't be quiet. . . . He's not gifted. Your son will never be able to focus on anything." Bob Bowman, his coach since age 11, reports that Michael spent a lot of time on the side of the pool by the lifeguard stand for disruptive behavior. That same misbehavior has cropped up from time to time in his adult life as well.

Yet, he's set dozens of world records. In 2004 he won six gold and two bronze medals in Athens and then, in 2008, a record eight in Beijing, surpassing the legendary Mark Spitz. His 18 gold medals set a record for Olympians in any sport. Before he hung up his goggles in retirement, his wins at the 2012 London Olympic Games brought his total medal count to 22 and earned him the status of most-decorated Olympian in any sport in history. Talking about Phelps, one reporter said, "If he were a country he'd be ranked 12th over the last three Olympics." Today, his mom reports, "Michael's ability to focus amazes me." Bowman calls it "his strongest attribute." How did this happen? How did the boy who would "never be able to focus on anything" achieve so much?

Phelps became a person of selected discipline.

From age 14 through the Beijing Olympics, Phelps trained seven days a week, 365 days a year. He figured that by training on Sundays he got a 52-training-day advantage on the competition. He spent up to six hours in the water each day. "Channeling his energy is one of his great strengths," said Bowman. Not to oversimplify, but it's not a stretch to say that Phelps channeled all of his energy into one discipline that developed into one habit—swimming daily.

The payoff from developing the right habit is pretty obvious. It gets you the success you're searching for. What sometimes gets overlooked, however, is an amazing windfall: it also simplifies your life. Your life gets clearer and less complicated because you know what you have to do well and you know what you don't. The fact of the matter is that aiming discipline at the right habit gives you license to be less disciplined in other areas. When you do the right thing, it can liberate you from having to monitor everything.

Michael Phelps found his sweet spot in the swimming pool. Over time, finding the discipline to do this formed the habit that changed his life.

SIXTY-SIX DAYS TO THE SWEET SPOT

Discipline and habit. Honestly, most people never really want to talk about these. And who can blame them? I don't either. The images these words conjure in our heads are of something hard and unpleasant. Just reading the words is exhausting. But there's good news. The right discipline goes a long way, and habits are hard only in the beginning. Over time, the habit you're after becomes easier and easier to sustain. It's true. Habits require much less energy and effort to maintain than to begin (see figure 7). Put up with the

THE ROLE of DISCIPLINE in ACHIEVEMENT

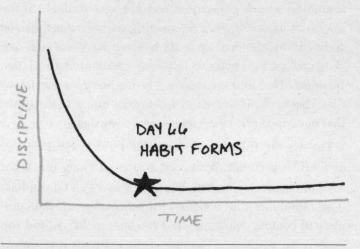

DISCIPLINE

DAY 66
HABIT FORMS

TIME

FIG. 7 Once a new behavior becomes a habit, it takes less discipline to maintain.

discipline long enough to turn it into a habit, and the journey feels different. Lock in one habit so it becomes part of your life, and you can effectively ride the routine with less wear and tear on yourself. The hard stuff becomes habit, and habit makes the hard stuff easy.

So, how long do you have to maintain discipline? Researchers at the University College of London have the answer. In 2009, they asked the question: How long does it take to establish a new habit? They were looking for the moment when a new behavior becomes automatic or ingrained. The point of "automaticity" came when participants were 95 percent through the power curve and the effort needed to sustain it was about as low as it would get. They asked students to take on exercise and diet goals for a period of time and monitor their progress. The results suggest that it takes an average of 66 days to acquire a new habit. The full range was 18 to 254 days, but the 66 days represented a sweet spot—with easier behaviors taking fewer days on average and tough ones taking longer. Self-help circles tend to preach that it takes 21 days to make a change, but modern science doesn't back that up. It takes time to develop the right habit, so don't give up too soon. Decide what the right one is, then give yourself all the time you need and apply all the discipline you can summon to develop it.

Australian researchers Megan Oaten and Ken Cheng have even found some evidence of a halo effect around habit creation. In their studies, students who successfully acquired one positive habit reported less stress; less impulsive spending; better dietary habits; decreased alcohol, tobacco, and caffeine consumption; fewer hours watching TV; and even fewer dirty dishes. Sustain the discipline long enough on one habit, and not only does it become easier, but so do other things as well. It's why those with the right habits seem to do better than others. They're doing the most important thing regularly and, as a result, everything else is easier.

BIG IDEAS

1. **Don't be a disciplined person.** Be a person of powerful habits and use selected discipline to develop them.

2. **Build one habit at a time.** Success is sequential, not simultaneous. No one actually has the discipline to acquire more than one powerful new habit at a time. Super-successful people aren't superhuman at all; they've just used selected discipline to develop a few significant habits. One at a time. Over time.

3. **Give each habit enough time.** Stick with the discipline long enough for it to become routine. Habits, on average, take 66 days to form. Once a habit is solidly established, you can either build on that habit or, if appropriate, build another one.

If you are what you repeatedly do, then achievement isn't an action you take but a habit you forge into your life. You don't have to seek out success. Harness the power of selected discipline to build the right habit, and extraordinary results will find you.

WILLPOWER IS ALWAYS ON WILL-CALL 7

Why would you ever do something the hard way? Why would you ever knowingly get behind the eight ball, deliberately crawl between a rock and a hard place, or intentionally work with one hand tied behind your back? You wouldn't. But most people unwittingly do every day. When we tie our success to our willpower without understanding what that really means, we set ourselves up for failure. And we don't have to.

"Odysseus understood how weak willpower actually is when he asked his crew to bind him to the mast while sailing by the seductive Sirens."

—Patricia Cohen

Often quoted as a statement about sheer determination, the old English proverb "Where there's a will, there's a way" has probably misled as many as it's helped. It just rolls off the tongue and passes so quickly through our head that few stop to hear its full meaning. Widely regarded as the singular source of personal strength, it gets misinterpreted as a cleverly phrased, one-dimensional prescription for success. But for will to have its most powerful way, there's more to it than that. Construe willpower as just a call for character and you miss its other equally essential element: timing. It's a critical piece.

For most of my life I never gave willpower much thought. Once I did, it captivated me. The ability to control oneself to determine one's actions is a pretty powerful idea. Base it on training and it's called discipline. But do it because you simply can, that's raw power. The power of will.

It seemed so straightforward: invoke my will and success was mine. I was on my way. Sadly, I didn't need to pack much, for it was a short trip. As I set out to impose my will against defenseless goals, I quickly discovered something discouraging: I didn't always have willpower. One moment I had it, the next—poof! I didn't. One day it was AWOL, the next—bang! It was at my beck and call. My willpower seemed to come and go as if it had a life of its own. Building success around full strength, on-demand willpower proved unsuccessful. My initial thought was, What's wrong with me? Was I a loser? Apparently so. It seemed I had no grit. No strength of character. No inner fortitude. Consequently, I gutted it up, bore down with determination, doubled my effort, and reached a humbling conclusion: willpower isn't on will-call. As powerful as my motivation was, my willpower wasn't just sitting around waiting for my call, ready at any moment to enforce my will on anything I wanted. I was taken aback. I had always assumed that it would always be there. That I could simply access it whenever I wanted, to get whatever I wanted. I was wrong.

Willpower is always on will-call is a lie.

Most people assume willpower matters, but many might not fully appreciate how critical it is to our success. One highly unusual research project revealed just how important it really is.

TODDLER TORTURE

In the late '60s and early '70s, researcher Walter Mischel began methodically tormenting four-year-olds at Stanford University's Bing Nursery School. More than 500 children were volunteered for the diabolical program by their own parents, many of whom would later, like millions of others, laugh mercilessly at videos of the squirming, miserable kids. The devilish experiment was called "The Marshmallow Test." It was an interesting way to look at willpower.

Kids were offered one of three treats—a pretzel, a cookie, or the now infamous marshmallow. The child was told that the researcher had to step away, and if he could wait 15 minutes until the researcher returned, he'd be awarded a second treat. One treat now or two later. (Mischel knew they'd designed the test well when a few of the kids wanted to quit as soon as they explained the ground rules.)

Left alone with a marshmallow they couldn't eat, kids engaged in all kinds of delay strategies, from closing their eyes, pulling their own hair, and turning away, to hovering over, smelling, and even caressing their treats. On average, kids held out less than three minutes. And only three out of ten managed to delay their gratification until the researcher returned. It was pretty apparent most kids struggled with delayed gratification. Willpower was in short supply.

Initially, no one assumed anything about what success or failure in the marshmallow test might say about a child's future. That insight came about organically. Mischel's three daughters attended Bing Nursery School, and over the next few years, he slowly began to see a pattern when he'd ask them about classmates who had participated in the experiment. Children who had successfully waited for the second treat seemed to be doing better. A lot better.

Starting in 1981, Mischel began systematically tracking down the original subjects. He requested transcripts, compiled records, and mailed questionnaires in an attempt to measure their relative academic and social progress. His hunch was correct—willpower or the ability to delay gratification was a huge indicator of future success. Over the next 30-plus years, Mischel and his colleagues published numerous papers on how "high delayers" fared better. Success in the experiment predicted higher general academic achievement, SAT test scores that were on average 210 points higher, higher feelings of self-worth, and better stress management. On the other hand, "low delayers" were 30 percent more likely to be overweight and later suffered higher rates of drug addiction. When your mother told you "all good things come to those who wait," she wasn't kidding.

Willpower is so important that using it effectively should be a high priority. Unfortunately, since it's not on will-call, putting it to its best use requires you to manage it. Just as with "the early bird gets the worm" and "make hay while the sun shines," willpower is a timing issue. *When* you have your will, you get your way. Although character is an essential element of willpower, the key to harnessing it is when you use it.

RENEWABLE ENERGY

Think of willpower like the power bar on your cell phone. Every morning you start out with a full charge. As the day goes on, every time you draw on it you're using it up. So as your green bar shrinks, so does your resolve, and when it eventually goes red, you're done. Willpower has a limited battery life but can be recharged with some downtime. It's a limited but renewable resource. Because you have a limited supply, each act of will creates a win-lose scenario where winning in an immediate situation through willpower makes you more likely to lose later because you have less of it. Make it through a tough day in the trenches, and the lure of late-night snacking can become your diet's downfall.

Everyone accepts that limited resources must be managed, yet we fail to recognize that willpower is one of them. We act as though our supply of willpower were endless. As a result, we don't consider it a personal resource to be managed, like food or sleep. This repeatedly puts us in a tight spot, for when we need our willpower the most, it may not be there.

Stanford University professor Baba Shiv's research shows just how fleeting our willpower can be. He divided 165 undergraduate students into two groups and asked them to memorize either a two-digit or a seven-digit number. Both tasks were well within the average person's cognitive abilities, and they could take as much time as they needed. When they were ready, students would then go to another room where they would recall the number. Along the way, they were offered a snack for participating in the study. The two choices were chocolate cake or a bowl of fruit salad—guilty pleasure or healthy treat. Here's the kicker: students asked to memorize the seven-digit number were nearly twice as likely to choose cake. This tiny extra cognitive load was just enough to prevent a prudent choice.

The implications are staggering. The more we use our mind, the less minding power we have. Willpower is like a fast-twitch muscle that gets tired and needs rest. It's incredibly powerful, but it has no endurance. As Kathleen Vohs put it in *Prevention* magazine in 2009, "Willpower is like gas in your car. . . . When you resist something tempting, you use some up. The more you resist, the emptier your tank gets, until you run out of gas." In fact, a measly five extra digits is all it takes to drain our willpower dry.

While decisions tap our willpower, the food we eat is also a key player in our level of willpower.

FOOD FOR THOUGHT

The brain makes up 1/50th of our body mass but consumes a staggering 1/5th of the calories we burn for energy. If your brain were a car, in terms of gas mileage, it'd be a Hummer. Most of our conscious activity is happening in our prefrontal cortex, the part of our brain responsible for focus, handling short-term memory, solving problems, and moderating impulse control. It's at the heart of what makes us human and the center for our executive control and willpower.

Here's an interesting fact. The "last in, first out" theory is very much at work inside our head. The most recent parts of our brain to develop are the first to suffer if there is a shortage of resources. Older, more developed areas of the brain, such as those that regulate breathing and our nervous responses, get first helpings from our blood stream and are virtually unaffected if we decide to skip a meal. The prefrontal cortex, on the other hand, feels the impact. Unfortunately, being relatively young in terms of human development, it's the runt of the litter come feeding time.

Advanced research shows us why this matters. A 2007 article in the *Journal of Personality and Social Psychology* detailed nine separate studies on the impact of nutrition and willpower. In one set, researchers assigned tasks that did or did not involve willpower and measured blood-sugar levels before and after each task. Participants who exercised willpower showed a marked drop in the levels of glucose in the bloodstream. Subsequent studies showed the impact on performance when two groups completed one willpower-related task and then did another. Between tasks, one group was given a glass of Kool-Aid lemonade sweetened with real sugar (buzz) and the other was given a placebo, lemonade with Splenda (buzzkill). The placebo group had roughly twice as many errors on the subsequent test as the sugar group.

The studies concluded that willpower is a mental muscle that doesn't bounce back quickly. If you employ it for one task, there will be less power available for the next unless you refuel. To do our best, we literally have to feed our minds, which gives new credence to the old saw, "food for thought." Foods that elevate blood sugar evenly over long periods, like complex carbohydrates and proteins, become the fuel of choice for high-achievers—literal proof that "you are what you eat."

DEFAULT JUDGMENT

One of the real challenges we have is that when our willpower is low we tend to fall back on our default settings. Researchers Jonathan Levav of the Stanford School of Business in California, along with Liora Avnaim-Pesso and Shai Danziger of Ben Gurion University of the Negev, found a creative way to investigate this. They took a hard look at the impact of willpower on the Israeli parole system.

The researchers analyzed 1,112 parole board hearings assigned to eight judges over a ten-month period (which incidentally amounted to 40 percent of Israel's total parole requests over that period). The pace is grueling. The judges hear arguments and take about six minutes to render a decision on 14 to 35 parole requests a day, and they get only two breaks—a morning snack and late lunch—to rest and refuel. The impact of their schedule is as spectacular as it is surprising: In the mornings and after each break, parolees' chances for being released peak at 65 percent, and then plunge to near zero by the end of each period (see figure 8).

The results are most likely tied to the mental toll of repetitive decision making. These are big decisions for the parolees and the public at large. High stakes and the assembly-line rhythm demand intense focus throughout the day. As their energy is spent, judges mentally collapse into their "default choice," which doesn't turn out so well for hopeful prisoners. The default decision for a parole judge is no. When in doubt and willpower is low, the prisoner stays behind bars.

And if you're not careful, your default settings may convict you too.

When our willpower runs out, we all revert to our default settings. This begs the question: *What are your default*

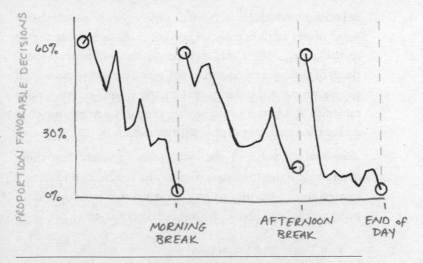

PROPORTION FAVORABLE DECISIONS

60%

30%

0%

MORNING BREAK

AFTERNOON BREAK

END of DAY

Good decisions depend on more than just wisdom and common sense.

settings? If your willpower is dragging, will you grab the bag of carrots or the bag of chips? Will you be up for focusing on the work at hand or down for any distraction that drops in? When your most important work is done while your willpower wanes, default will define your level of achievement. Average is often the result.

GIVE WILLPOWER THE TIME OF DAY

We lose our willpower not because we think about it but because we don't. Without appreciating that it can come and go, we let it do exactly that. Without intentionally protecting it every day, we allow ourselves to go from a will and a way to no will and no way. If success is what we're after, this won't work.

Think about it. There are degrees of willpower strength. Like the battery indicator going from green to red, there is willpower and there is "won't" power. Most people bring won't power to their most important challenges without ever realizing that's what makes them so hard. When we don't think of resolve as a resource that gets used up, when we fail to reserve it for the things that matter most, when we don't replenish it when it's low, we are probably setting ourselves up for the toughest possible path to success.

So how do you put your willpower to work? You think about it. Pay attention to it. Respect it. You make doing what matters most a priority when your willpower is its highest. In other words, you give it the time of day it deserves.

WHAT TAXES YOUR WILLPOWER

- Implementing new behaviors
- Filtering distractions
- Resisting temptation
- Suppressing emotion
- Restraining aggression
- Suppressing impulses
- Taking tests
- Trying to impress others
- Coping with fear
- Doing something you don't enjoy
- Selecting long-term over short-term rewards

Every day, without realizing it, we engage in all manner of activities that diminish our willpower. Willpower is depleted when we make decisions to focus our attention, suppress our feelings and impulses, or modify our behavior in pursuit of goals. It's like taking an ice pick and gouging a hole in our gas line. Before long we have willpower leaking everywhere and none left to do our most important work. So like any other limited but vital resource, willpower must be managed.

When it comes to willpower, timing is everything. You will need your willpower at full strength to ensure that when you're doing the right thing, you don't let anything distract you or steer you away from it. Then you need enough willpower the rest of the day to either support or avoid sabotaging what you've done. That's all the willpower you need to be successful. So, if you want to get the most out of your day, do your most important work—your ONE Thing—early, before your willpower is drawn down. Since your self-control will be sapped throughout the day, use it when it's at full strength on what matters most.

BIG IDEAS

1. **Don't spread your willpower too thin.** On any given day, you have a limited supply of willpower, so decide what matters and reserve your willpower for it.

2. **Monitor your fuel gauge.** Full-strength willpower requires a full tank. Never let what matters most be compromised simply because your brain was under-fueled. Eat right and regularly.

3. **Time your task.** Do what matters most first each day when your willpower is strongest. Maximum strength willpower means maximum success.

Don't fight your willpower. Build your days around how it works and let it do its part to build your life. Willpower may not be on willcall, but when you use it first on what matters most, you can always count on it.

8 A BALANCED LIFE

"The truth is, balance is bunk. It is an unattainable pipe dream. . . . The quest for balance between work and life, as we've come to think of it, isn't just a losing proposition; it's a hurtful, destructive one."

—Keith H. Hammonds

Nothing ever achieves absolute balance. Nothing. No matter how imperceptible it might be, what appears to be a state of balance is something entirely different—an act of *balancing*. Viewed wistfully as a noun, balance is lived practically as a verb. Seen as something we ultimately attain, balance is actually something we constantly do. A "balanced life" is a myth—a misleading concept most accept as a worthy and attainable goal without ever stopping to truly consider it. I want you to consider it. I want you to challenge it. I want you to reject it.

A balanced life is a lie.

The idea of balance is exactly that—an idea. In philosophy, "the golden mean" is the moderate middle between polar extremes, a concept used to describe a place between two positions that is more desirable than one state or the other. This is a grand idea, but not a very practical one. Idealistic, but not realistic. Balance doesn't exist.

This is tough to conceive, much less believe, mainly because one of the most frequent laments is "I need more balance," a common mantra for what's missing in most lives. We hear about balance so much we automatically assume it's exactly what we should be seeking. It's not. Purpose, meaning, significance—these are what make a successful life. Seek them and you will most certainly live your life out of balance, crisscrossing an invisible middle line as you pursue your priorities. The act of living a full life by giving time to what matters is a balancing act. Extraordinary results require focused attention and time. Time on one thing means time away from another. This makes balance impossible.

THE GENESIS OF A MYTH

Historically, balancing our lives is a novel privilege to even consider. For thousands of years, work was life. If you didn't work—hunt game, harvest crops, or raise livestock—you didn't live long. But things changed. Jared Diamond's Pulitzer Prize–winning *Guns, Germs, and Steel: The Fates of Human Societies* illustrates how farm-based societies that generated a surplus of food ultimately gave rise to professional specialization. "Twelve thousand years ago, everybody on earth was a hunter-gatherer; now almost all of us are farmers or else are fed by farmers." This freedom from having to forage or farm allowed people to become scholars and craftsmen. Some worked to put food on our tables while others built the tables.

At first, most people worked according to their needs and ambitions. The blacksmith didn't have to stay at the forge until 5 P.M.; he could go home when the horse's feet were shod. Then 19th-century industrialization saw for the first time large numbers working for someone else. The story became one of hard-driving bosses, year-round work schedules, and lighted factories that ignored dawn and dusk. Consequently, the 20th century witnessed the start of significant grassroots movements to protect workers and limit work hours.

Still, the term "work-life balance" wasn't coined until the mid-1980s when more than half of all married women joined the workforce. To paraphrase Ralph E. Gomory's preface in the 2005 book *Being Together, Working Apart: Dual-Career Families and the Work-Life Balance,* we went from a family unit with a breadwinner and a homemaker to one with two breadwinners and no homemaker. Anyone with a pulse knows who got stuck with the extra work in the beginning. However, by the '90s "work-life balance" had quickly become a common watchword for men too. A LexisNexis survey of the top 100 newspapers and magazines around the world shows a dramatic rise in the number of articles on the topic, from 32 in the decade from 1986 to 1996 to a high of 1,674 articles in 2007 alone (see figure 9).

It's probably not a coincidence that the ramp-up of technology parallels the rise in the belief that something is missing in our lives. Infiltrated space and fewer boundaries will do that.

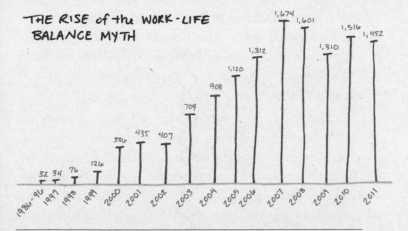

THE RISE of the WORK-LIFE BALANCE MYTH

1,674   1,601
1,516 1,452
1,312
1,310
1,120
908
709
435 407
386
126
32 34 76

1980-96 1997 1998 1999 2000 2001 2002 2003 2004 2005 2006 2007 2008 2009 2010 2011

FIG. 9 The number of times "work-life balance" is mentioned in newspaper and magazine articles has exploded in recent years.

Rooted in real-life challenges, the idea of "work-life balance" has clearly captured our minds and imagination.

MIDDLE MISMANAGEMENT

The desire for balance makes sense. Enough time for everything and everything done in time. It sounds so appealing that just thinking about it makes us feel serene and peaceful. This calm is so real that we just know it's the way life was meant to be. But it's not.

If you think of balance as the middle, then out of balance is when you're away from it. Get too far away from the middle and you're living at the extremes. The problem with living in the middle is that it prevents you from making extraordinary time commitments to anything. In your effort to attend to all things, everything gets shortchanged and nothing gets its due.

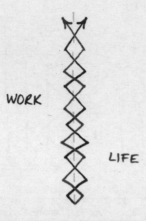

WORK-LIFE in the MIDDLE

WORK

LIFE

FIG. 10 Pursuing a balanced life means never pursuing anything at the extremes.

Sometimes this can be okay and sometimes not. Knowing when to pursue the middle and when to pursue the extremes is in essence the true beginning of wisdom. Extraordinary results are achieved by this negotiation with your time.

The reason we shouldn't pursue balance is that the magic never happens in the middle; magic happens at the extremes. The dilemma is that chasing the extremes presents real challenges. We naturally understand that success lies at the outer edges, but we don't know how to manage our lives while we're out there.

When we work too long, eventually our personal life suffers. Falling prey to the belief that long hours are virtuous, we unfairly blame work when we say, "I have no life." Often, it's just the opposite. Even if our work life doesn't interfere, our personal life itself can be so full of "have-tos" that we

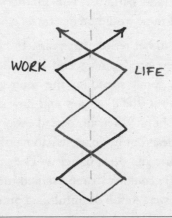

WORK-LIFE at the EXTREMES

FIG. 11 Pursuing the extremes presents its own set of problems.

again reach the same defeated conclusion: "I have no life." And sometimes we get hit from both sides. Some of us face so many personal and professional demands that everything suffers. Breakdown imminent, we once again declare, "I have no life!"

Just like playing to the middle, playing to the extremes is the kind of middle mismanagement that plays out all the time.

TIME WAITS FOR NO ONE

My wife once told me the story of a friend of hers. The friend's mother was a schoolteacher and her father was a farmer. They had scrimped, saved, and done with less their entire lives in anticipation of retirement and travel. The woman fondly remembered the regular shopping trips she and her mother would take to the local fabric store where they would pick out some fabric and patterns. The mother explained that when she retired these would be her travel clothes.

She never got to her retirement years. In her final year of teaching, she developed cancer and later died. The father never felt good about spending the money they'd saved, believing that it was "their" money and now she wasn't there to share it with him. When he passed away and my wife's friend went to clean out her parents' home, she discovered a closet full of fabric and dress patterns. The father had never cleaned it out. He couldn't. It represented too much. It was as if its contents were so full of unfulfilled promises that they were too heavy to lift.

Time waits for no one. Push something to an extreme and postponement can become permanent.

I once knew a highly successful businessman who had worked long days and weekends for most of his life, sincere in his belief that he was doing it all for his family. Someday, when he was done, they would all enjoy the fruits of his labor, spend time together, travel, and do all the things they'd never done. After giving many years to building his company, he had recently sold it and was open to discussing what he might do next. I asked him how he was doing and he proudly proclaimed that he was fine. "When I was building the business, I was never home and rarely saw my family. So now I'm with them on vacation making up for lost time. You know how it is, right? Now that I have the money and the time, I'm getting those years back."

Do you really think you can ever get back a child's bedtime story or birthday? Is a party for a five-year-old with imaginary pals the same as dinner with a teenager with high-school friends? Is an adult attending a young child's soccer game on par with attending a soccer game with an adult child? Do you think you can cut a deal with God that time stands still for you, holding off on anything important until you're ready to participate again?

When you gamble with your time, you may be placing a bet you can't cover. Even if you're sure you can win, be careful that you can live with what you lose.

Toying with time will lead you down a rabbit hole with no way out. Believing this lie does its harm by convincing you to do things you shouldn't and stop doing things you should. Middle mismanagement can be one of the most destructive things you ever do. You can't ignore the inevitability of time.

So if achieving balance is a lie, then what do you do? Counterbalance.

Replace the word "balance" with "counterbalance" and what you experience makes sense. The things we presume to have balance are really just counterbalancing. The ballerina is a classic example. When the ballerina poses *en pointe,* she can appear weightless, floating on air, the very idea of balance and grace. A closer look would reveal her toe shoes vibrating rapidly, making minute adjustments for balance. Counterbalancing done well gives the illusion of balance.

COUNTERBALANCING—THE LONG AND SHORT OF IT

When we say we're out of balance, we're usually referring to a sense that some priorities—things that matter to us—are being underserved or unmet. The problem is that when you focus on what is truly important, something will always be underserved. No matter how hard you try, there will always be things left undone at the end of your day, week, month, year, and life. Trying to get them all done is folly. When the things that matter most get done, you'll still be left with a sense of things being undone—a sense of imbalance. Leaving some things undone is a necessary tradeoff for extraordinary results. But you can't leave everything undone, and that's where counterbalancing comes in. The idea of counterbalancing is that you never go so far that you can't find your way back or stay so long that there is nothing waiting for you when you return.

This is so important that your very life may hang in the balance. An 11-year study of nearly 7,100 British civil servants concluded that habitual long hours can be deadly. Researchers showed that individuals who worked more than 11 hours a day (a 55-plus hour workweek) were 67 percent more likely to suffer from heart disease. Counterbalancing is not only about your sense of well-being, it's essential to your being well.

WORK-LIFE COUNTERBALANCING

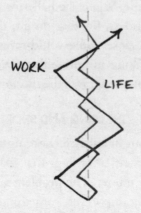

FIG. 12 Extraordinary results at work require longer periods between counterbalancing.

There are two types of counterbalancing: the balancing between work and personal life and the balancing within each. In the world of professional success, it's not about how much overtime you put in; the key ingredient is focused time over time. To achieve an extraordinary result you must choose what matters most and give it all the time it demands. This requires getting extremely out of balance in relation to all other work issues, with only infrequent counterbalancing to address them. In your personal world, awareness is the essential ingredient. Awareness of your spirit and body, awareness of your family and friends, awareness of your personal needs—none of these can be sacrificed if you intend to "have a life," so you can never forsake them for work or one for the other. You can move back and forth quickly between these and often even combine the activities around them, but you can't neglect any of them for long. Your personal life requires tight counterbalancing.

Whether or not to go out of balance isn't really the question. The question is: "Do you go short or long?" In your personal life, go short and avoid long periods where you're out of balance. Going short lets you stay connected to all the things that matter most and move them along together. In your professional life, go long and make peace with the idea that the pursuit of extraordinary results may require you to be out of balance for long periods. Going long allows you to focus on what matters most, even at the expense of other, lesser priorities. In your personal life, nothing gets left behind. At work it's required.

In his novel *Suzanne's Diary for Nicholas,* James Patterson artfully highlights where our priorities lie in our personal and professional balancing act: "Imagine life is a game in which you are juggling five balls. The balls are called work, family, health, friends, and integrity. And you're keeping all of them in the air. But one day you finally come to understand that work is a rubber ball. If you drop it, it will bounce back. The other four balls—family, health, friends, integrity—are made of glass. If you drop one of these, it will be irrevocably scuffed, nicked, perhaps even shattered."

LIFE IS A BALANCING ACT

The question of balance is really a question of priority. When you change your language from balancing to prioritizing, you see your choices more clearly and open the door to changing your destiny. Extraordinary results demand that you set a priority and act on it. When you act on your priority, you'll automatically go out of balance, giving more time to one thing over another. The challenge then doesn't become one of not going out of balance, for in fact you must. The challenge becomes how long you stay on your priority. To be able to address your priorities outside of work, be clear about your most important work priority so you can get it done. Then go home and be clear about your priorities there so you can get back to work.

When you're supposed to be working, work, and when you're supposed to be playing, play. It's a weird tightrope you're walking, but it's only when you get your priorities mixed up that things fall apart.

1. **Think about two balancing buckets.** Separate your work life and personal life into two distinct buckets—not to compartmentalize them, just for counterbalancing. Each has its own counterbalancing goals and approaches.

2. **Counterbalance your work bucket.** View work as involving a skill or knowledge that must be mastered. This will cause you to give disproportionate time to your ONE Thing and will throw the rest of your work day, week, month, and year continually out of balance. Your work life is divided into two distinct areas—what matters most and everything else. You will have to take what matters to the extremes and be okay with what happens to the rest. Professional success requires it.

3. **Counterbalance your personal life bucket.** Acknowledge that your life actually has multiple areas and that each requires a minimum of attention for you to feel that you "have a life." Drop any one and you will feel the effects. This requires constant awareness. You must never go too long or too far without counterbalancing them so that they are all active areas of your life. Your personal life requires it.

Start leading a counterbalanced life. Let the right things take precedence when they should and get to the rest when you can.

An extraordinary life is a counterbalancing act.

9 BIG IS BAD

The Big Bad Wolf. Big Bad John. From folktales to folk songs, the suggestion that big and bad go together has been a common theme across history—so much so that many think they're synonymous. They're not. Big can be bad and bad can be big, but they're not one and the same. They aren't inherently related.

A big opportunity is better than a small one, but a small problem is better than a big one. Sometimes you want the biggest present under the tree and sometimes you want the smallest. Often a big laugh or a big cry is just what you need, and every so often a small chuckle and a few tears will do the trick. Big and bad are no more tied together than small and good.

Big is bad is a lie.

It's quite possibly the worst lie of all, for if you fear big success, you'll either avoid it or sabotage your efforts to achieve it.

WHO'S AFRAID OF THE BIG BAD BIG?

Place big and results in the same room and a lot of people balk or walk. Mention big with achievement and their first thoughts are *hard*, *complicated*, and *time-consuming*. *Difficult to get there* and *complex once you do* pretty much sums up their views. *Overwhelming* and *intimidating* is what they feel. For some reason there is the fear that big success brings crushing pressure and stress, that the pursuit of it robs them of not only time with family and friends but eventually their health. Uncertain of the right to achieve big, or fearful of what might happen if they try and fall short, their head spins just thinking about it and they immediately doubt they have a head for heights.

All of this reinforces a "dis-ease" with the very idea of big. To invent a word, call it *megaphobia*—the irrational fear of big.

When we connect big with bad, we trigger shrinking thinking. Lowering our trajectory feels safe. Staying where we are feels prudent. But the opposite is true: When big is believed to be bad, small thinking rules the day and big never sees the light of it.

FLAT WRONG

How many ships didn't sail because of the belief that the earth was flat? How much progress was impeded because man wasn't supposed to breathe underwater, fly through the air, or venture into outer space? Historically, we've done a remarkably poor job of estimating our limits. The good news is that science isn't about guessing, but rather the art of progressing.

And so is your life.

None of us knows our limits. Borders and boundaries may be clear on a map, but when we apply them to our lives, the lines aren't so apparent. I was once asked if I thought thinking big was realistic. I paused to reflect on this and then said, "Let me ask you a question first: Do you know what your limits are?" "No," was the reply. So I said that it seemed the question was irrelevant. No one knows their ultimate ceiling for achievement, so worrying about it is a waste of time. What if someone told you that you could never achieve above a certain level? That you were required to pick an upper limit which you could never exceed? What would you pick? A low one or a high one? I think we know the answer. Put in this situation, we would all do the same thing—go big. Why? Because you wouldn't want to limit yourself.

When you allow yourself to accept that big is about who you can become, you look at it differently.

In this context, big is a placeholder for what you might call a leap of possibility. It's the office intern visualizing the boardroom or a penniless immigrant imagining a business revolution. It's about bold ideas that might threaten your comfort zones but simultaneously reflect your greatest opportunities. Believing in big frees you to ask different questions, follow different paths, and try new things. This opens the doors to possibilities that until now only lived inside you.

Sabeer Bhatia arrived in America with only $250 in his pocket, but he wasn't alone. Sabeer came with big plans and the belief that he could grow a business faster than any business in history. And he did. He created Hotmail. Microsoft, a witness to Hotmail's meteoric rise, eventually bought it for $400 million.

According to his mentor, Farouk Arjani, Sabeer's success was directly related to his ability to think big. "What set Sabeer apart from the hundreds of entrepreneurs I've met is the gargantuan size of his dream. Even before he had a product, before he had any money behind him, he was completely convinced that he was going to build a major company that would be worth hundreds of millions of dollars. He had an unrelenting conviction that he was not just going to build a run-of-the-mill Silicon Valley company. But over time I realized, by golly, he was probably going to pull it off."

As of 2011, Hotmail ranked as one of the most successful webmail service providers in the world, with more than 360 million active users.

GOING BIG

Thinking big is essential to extraordinary results. Success requires action, and action requires thought. But here's the catch—the only actions that become springboards to succeeding big are those informed by big thinking to begin with. Make this connection, and the importance of how big you think begins to sink in.

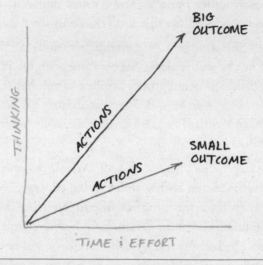

THINK BIG — ACT BIG — SUCCEED BIG

BIG OUTCOME

THINKING

ACTIONS

SMALL OUTCOME

ACTIONS

TIME : EFFORT

FIG. 13 Thinking informs actions and actions determine outcomes.

Everyone has the same amount of time, and hard work is simply hard work. As a result, what you do in the time you work determines what you achieve. And since what you do is determined by what you think, how big you think becomes the launching pad for how high you achieve.

Think of it this way. Every level of achievement requires its own combination of what you do, how you do it, and who you do it with. The trouble is that the combination of what, how, and who that gets you to one level of success won't naturally evolve to a better combination that leads to the next level of success. Doing something one way doesn't always lay the foundation for doing something better, nor does a relationship with one person automatically set the stage for a more successful relationship with another. It's unfortunate, but these things don't build on each other. If you learn to do something one way, and with one set of relationships, that may work fine until you want to achieve more. It's then that you'll discover you've created an artificial ceiling of achievement for yourself that may be too hard to break through. In effect, you've boxed yourself in when there is a simple way to avoid it. Think as big as you possibly can and base what you do, how you do it, and who you do it with on succeeding at that level. It just might take you more than your lifetime to run into the walls of a box this big.

When people talk about "reinventing" their career or their business, small boxes are often the root cause. 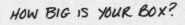What you build today will either empower or restrict you tomorrow. It

FIG. 14 Choose your box—choose your outcome.

> "The rung of a ladder was never meant to rest upon, but only to hold a man's foot long enough to enable him to put the other somewhat higher."
>
> —Thomas Henry Huxley

will either serve as a platform for the next level of your success or as a box, trapping you where you are.

Big gives you the best chance for extraordinary results today and tomorrow. When Arthur Guinness set up his first brewery, he signed a 9,000-year lease. When J. K. Rowling conceived Harry Potter, she thought big and envisioned seven years at Hogwarts before she penned the first chapter of the first of seven books. Before Sam Walton opened the first Wal-Mart, he envisioned a business so big that he felt he needed to go ahead and set up his future estate plan to minimize inheritance taxes. By thinking big, long before he made it big, he was able to save his family an estimated $11 to $13 billion in estate taxes. Transferring the wealth of one of the greatest companies ever built as tax-free as possible requires thinking big from the beginning.

Thinking big isn't just about business. Candace Lightner started Mothers Against Drunk Driving in 1980 after her daughter was killed in a hit-and-run accident by a drunk driver. Today, MADD has saved more than 300,000 lives. As a six-year-old in 1998, Ryan Hreljac was inspired by stories told by his teacher to help bring clean water to Africa. Today his foundation, Ryan's Well, has improved conditions and helped bring safe water to over 750,000 people in 16 countries. Derreck Kayongo recognized both the waste and hidden value in getting new soap into hotels every day. So in 2009 he created the Global Soap Project, which has provided more than 250,000 bars of soap in 21 countries, helping combat child mortality by simply giving impoverished people the chance to wash their hands.

Asking big questions can be daunting. Big goals can seem unattainable at first. Yet how many times have you set out to do something that seemed like a real stretch at the time, only to discover it was much easier than you thought? Sometimes things are easier than we imagine, and truthfully sometimes they're a lot harder. That's when it's important to realize that on the journey to achieving big, you get bigger. Big requires growth, and by the time you arrive, you're big too! What seemed an insurmountable mountain from a distance is just a small hill when you arrive—at least in proportion to the person you've become. Your thinking, your skills, your relationships, your sense of what is possible and what it takes all grow on the journey to big.

As you experience big, you become big.

THE BIG DEAL

For more than four decades, Stanford psychologist Carol S. Dweck has studied the science of how our self-conceptions influence our actions. Her work offers great insight into why thinking big is such a big deal.

Dweck's work with children revealed two mindsets in action—a "growth" mindset that generally thinks big and seeks growth and a "fixed" mindset that places artificial limits and avoids failure. Growth-minded students, as she calls them, employ better learning strategies, experience less helplessness, exhibit more positive effort, and achieve more in the classroom than their fixed-minded peers. They are less likely to place limits on their lives and more likely to reach for their potential. Dweck points out that mindsets can and do change. Like any other habit, you set your mind to it until the right mindset becomes routine.

When Scott Forstall started recruiting talent to his newly formed team, he warned that the top-secret project would provide ample opportunities to "make mistakes and struggle, but eventually we may do something that we'll remember the rest of our lives." He gave this curious pitch to superstars across the company, but only took those who *immediately* jumped at the challenge. He was looking for "growth-minded" people, as he later shared with Dweck after reading her book. Why is this significant? While you've probably never even heard of Forstall, you've certainly heard of what his team created. Forstall was a senior vice president at Apple, and the team he formed created the iPhone.

BLOWING UP YOUR LIFE

Big stands for greatness—extraordinary results. Pursue a big life and you're pursuing the greatest life you can possibly live. To live great, you have to think big. You must be open to the possibility that your life and what you accomplish can become great. Achievement and abundance show up because they're the natural outcomes of doing the right things with no limits attached.

Don't fear big. Fear mediocrity. Fear waste. Fear the lack of living to your fullest. When we fear big, we either consciously or subconsciously work against it. We either run toward lesser outcomes and opportunities or we simply run away from the big ones. If courage isn't the absence of fear, but moving past it, then thinking big isn't the absence of doubts, but moving past them. Only living big will let you experience your true life and work potential.

1. **Think big.** Avoid incremental thinking that simply asks, "What do I do next?" This is at best the slow lane to success and, at worst, the off ramp. Ask bigger questions. A good rule of thumb is to double down everywhere in your life. If your goal is ten, ask the question: "How can I reach 20?" Set a goal so far above what you want that you'll be building a plan that practically guarantees your original goal.

2. **Don't order from the menu.** Apple's celebrated 1997 "Think Different" ad campaign featured icons like Ali, Dylan, Einstein, Hitchcock, Picasso, Gandhi, and others who "saw things differently" and who went on to transform the world we know. The point was that they didn't choose from the available options; they imagined outcomes that no one else had. They ignored the menu and ordered their own creations. As the ad reminds us, *"People who are crazy enough to think they can change the world are the only ones who do."*

3. **Act bold.** Big thoughts go nowhere without bold action. Once you've asked a big question, pause to imagine what life looks like with the answer. If you still can't imagine it, go study people who have already achieved it. What are the models, systems, habits, and relationships of other people who have found the answer? As much as we'd like to believe we're all different, what consistently works for others will almost always work for us.

4. **Don't fear failure.** It's as much a part of your journey to extraordinary results as success. Adopt a growth

mindset, and don't be afraid of where it can take you. Extraordinary results aren't built solely on extraordinary results. They're built on failure too. In fact, it would be accurate to say that we fail our way to success. When we fail, we stop, ask what we need to do to succeed, learn from our mistakes, and grow. Don't be afraid to fail. See it as part of your learning process and keep striving for your true potential.

Don't let small thinking cut your life down to size. Think big, aim high, act bold. And see just how big you can blow up your life.

PART

2

THE TRUTH
THE SIMPLE PATH TO PRODUCTIVITY

> "Be careful how
> you interpret the world;
> it *is* like that."
>
> —*Erich Heller*

UNCLENCHED

For many years, I suffered from trying to live the lies of success.

I began my career assuming everything mattered equally, so in an effort to cram it all in, I attempted too much at once. Frustrated, I eventually began to doubt I had the discipline or will to achieve success at all. As my life continually fell out of balance, I started to consider that trying to live a big life might be a bad thing. When you try to live up to something that isn't possible, you can get pretty down.

I was pretty down.

In an attempt to make it all work, I began to bear down even harder. You might say that I started to clench my way to success. I really did. I thought that this might be the way you went through life—with your jaw clenched, your fist clenched, your stomach clenched, and your butt clenched. Leaning forward, breath held and body taut, tight and totally tense. I just assumed that was the feeling of focus and intensity as I struggled to live with the lies. That approach actually worked, but it also put me in the hospital.

I also began to think you had to talk like a success, walk like a success, and even dress for success. It wasn't me, but I was open to any way to make things work, so I took seriously the suggestion that you are supposed to project the way you want to be. That approach worked as well, but after a while, I simply got tired of "playing" success.

I bought into getting up before the crack of dawn, getting revved up playing inspirational theme songs, and getting going before anyone else. In fact, I became so full of this thinking that I would drive to the office while the rest of the city slept and then crash at my desk just to make sure that I beat everyone else to work. I started to accept the notion that maybe this is what ambition and achievement looked like as I fought the good fight. I would hold staff meetings at 7:30 in the morning and, at 7:31, would actually shut the door and lock out anyone who showed up late. I was going overboard, but I was beginning to believe this was the only way you could succeed, and the way you pushed others to succeed as well. This approach also worked, but in the end it also pushed me too hard, others too far, and my world over the edge.

I was truly beginning to think that the secret to success was to get as tightly wound up as possible each morning, set myself on fire, and then open the door and fly through the day, unwinding on the world, until I literally burnt out.

And what did all of this get me? It got me success, and it got me sick. Eventually, it got me sick of success.

So what did I do? I ditched the lies and went in the opposite direction. I joined overachievers anonymous and went antiestablishment on all the success "tactics" that supposedly build success.

First off, I got unclenched. I actually started listening to my body, slowed down, and chilled out. Next, I started wearing T-shirts and jeans to work and defied anyone to make a comment. I dropped the language and the attitude and went back to just being me. I had breakfast with my family. I got in shape physically and spiritually and stayed there. And last, I started doing less. Yes, less. Intentionally, purposefully less. I was looser than ever, way laid back for me, and breathing. I challenged the axioms of success, and guess what? I became more successful than I ever dreamed possible and felt better than I'd ever felt in my life.

Here's what I found out: We overthink, overplan, and overanalyze our careers, our businesses, and our lives; that long hours are neither virtuous nor healthy; and that we usually succeed *in spite* of most of what we do, not *because* of it. I discovered that we can't manage time, and that the key to success isn't in all the things we do but in the handful of things we do well.

I learned that success comes down to this: being appropriate in the moments of your life. If you can honestly say,

"This is where I'm meant to be right now, doing exactly what I'm doing," then all the amazing possibilities for your life become possible.

Most of all, I learned that the ONE Thing is the surprisingly simple truth behind extraordinary results.

10 THE FOCUSING QUESTION

"There is an art to clearing away the clutter and focusing on what matters most. It is simple and it is transferable. It just requires the courage to take a different approach."

—George Anders

On June 23, 1885, in the town of Pittsburgh, Pennsylvania, Andrew Carnegie addressed the students of the Curry Commercial College. At the height of his business success, the Carnegie Steel Company was the largest and most profitable industrial enterprise in the world. Carnegie would later become the second-richest man in history, after John D. Rockefeller. In Carnegie's talk, entitled "The Road to Business Success," he discussed his life as a successful businessperson and gave this advice:

> And here is the prime condition of success, the great secret—concentrate your energy, thought and capital exclusively upon the business in which you are engaged. Having begun on one line, resolve to fight it out on that line, to lead in it, adopt every improvement, have the best machinery, and know the most about it. The concerns which fail are those which have scattered their capital, which means that they have scattered their brains also. They have investments in this, or that, or the other, here, there and everywhere. "Don't put all your eggs in one basket" is all wrong. I tell you "put all your eggs in one basket, and then watch that basket." Look round you and take notice; men who do that do not often fail. It is easy to watch and carry the one basket. It is trying to carry too many baskets that breaks most eggs in this country.

So, how do you know which basket to pick? The Focusing Question.

Mark Twain agreed with Carnegie and described it this way:

> The secret of getting ahead is getting started. The secret to getting started is breaking your complex overwhelming tasks into small manageable tasks and then starting on the first one.

So, how do you know what the first one should be? The Focusing Question.

Did you notice that both of these great men considered their advice a "secret"? I don't think it's so much a secret as something people know but don't give proper weight or importance.

Most people are familiar with the Chinese proverb "A journey of a thousand miles must begin with a single step." They just never stop to fully appreciate that if this is true, then the wrong first step begins a journey that could end as far as two thousand miles from where they want to be. The Focusing Question helps keep your first step from being a misstep.

LIFE IS A QUESTION

You may be asking, "Why focus on a question when what we really crave is an answer?" It's simple. Answers come from questions, and the quality of any answer is directly determined by the quality of the question. Ask the wrong question, get the wrong answer. Ask the right question, get the right answer. Ask the most powerful question possible, and the answer can be life altering.

Voltaire once wrote, "Judge a man by his questions rather than his answers." Sir Francis Bacon added, "A prudent question is one-half of wisdom." Indira Gandhi concluded that "the power to question is the basis of all human progress." Great questions are clearly the quickest path to great answers. Every discoverer and inventor begins his quest with a transformative question. The scientific method asks questions of the universe in hypothesis form. The more than 2,000-year-old Socratic Method, teaching through questions, is still embraced by educators from the heights of Harvard Law School to the local kindergarten class. Questions engage our critical thinking. Research shows that asking questions improves learning and performance by as much as 150 percent. In the end, it's hard to argue with author Nancy Willard, who wrote, "Sometimes questions are more important than answers."

I first became aware of the power of questions as a young man. I read a poem that affected me profoundly and I've carried it with me ever since.

MY WAGE

By J. B. Rittenhouse

I bargained with Life for a penny,

And Life would pay no more,

However I begged at evening

When I counted my scanty store.

For Life is a just employer,

He gives you what you ask,

But once you have set the wages,

Why, you must bear the task.

I worked for a menial's hire,

Only to learn, dismayed,

That any wage I had asked of Life,

Life would have willingly paid.

The last two lines deserve repeating: ". . . any wage I had asked of Life, Life would have willingly paid." One of the most empowering moments of my life came when I realized that life is a question and how we live it is our answer. How we phrase the questions we ask ourselves determines the answers that eventually become our life.

The challenge is that the right question isn't always so obvious. Most things we want don't come with a road map or a set of instructions, so it can be difficult to frame the right question. Clarity must come from us. It seems we must envision our own journeys, make our own maps, and create our own compasses. To get the answers we seek, we have to invent the right questions—and we're left to devise our own. So how do you do this? How do you come up with uncommon questions that take you to uncommon answers?

You ask one question: the Focusing Question.

Anyone who dreams of an uncommon life eventually discovers there is no choice but to seek an uncommon approach to living it. The Focusing Question is that uncommon approach. In a world of no instructions, it becomes the simple formula for finding exceptional answers that lead to extraordinary results.

What's the ONE Thing I can do
such that by doing it
everything else will be easier or
unnecessary?

The Focusing Question is so deceptively simple that its power is easily dismissed by anyone who doesn't closely examine it. But that would be a mistake. The Focusing Question can lead you to answer not only "big picture" questions (Where am I going? What target should I aim for?) but also "small focus" ones as well (What must I do right now to be on the path to getting the big picture? Where's the

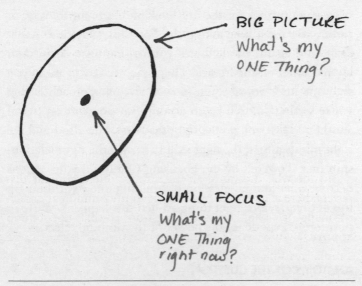

BIG PICTURE
What's my
ONE Thing?

SMALL FOCUS
What's my
ONE Thing
right now?

FIG. 15 The Focusing Question is a big-picture map and small-focus compass.

bull's-eye?). It tells you not only what your basket should be, but also the first step toward getting it. It shows you how big your life can be and just how small you must go to get there. It's both a map for the big picture and a compass for your smallest next move.

Extraordinary results are rarely happenstance. They come from the choices we make and the actions we take. The Focusing Question always aims you at the absolute best of both by forcing you to do what is essential to success—make a decision. But not just any decision—it drives you to make the best decision. It ignores what is doable and drills down to what is necessary, to what matters.

It leads you to the first domino.

To stay on track for the best possible day, month, year, or career, you must keep asking the Focusing Question. Ask it again and again, and it forces you to line up tasks in their levered order of importance. Then, each time you ask it, you see your next priority. The power of this approach is that you're setting yourself up to accomplish one task on top of another. When you do the right task first, you also build the right mindset first, the right skill first, and the right relationship first. Powered by the Focusing Question, your actions become a natural progression of building one right thing on top of the previous right thing. When this happens, you're in position to experience the power of the domino effect.

ANATOMY OF THE QUESTION

The Focusing Question collapses all possible questions into one: "What's the ONE Thing I can do / such that by doing it / everything else will be easier or unnecessary?"

PART ONE: "WHAT'S THE ONE THING I CAN DO . . ."

This sparks focused action. "What's the ONE Thing" tells you the answer will be one thing versus many. It forces you toward something specific. It tells you right up front that, although you may consider many options, you need to take this seriously because you don't get two, three, four, or more. You can't hedge your bet. You're allowed to pick one thing and one thing only.

The last phrase, "can do," is an embedded command directing you to take action that is possible. People often want to change this to "should do," "could do," or "would do," but those choices all miss the point. There are many things we should, could, or would do but never do. Action you "can do" beats intention every time.

PART TWO: ". . . SUCH THAT BY DOING IT . . ."

This tells you there's a criterion your answer must meet. It's the bridge between just doing something and doing something for a specific purpose. "Such that by doing it" lets you know you're going to have to dig deep, because when you do this ONE Thing, something else is going to happen.

> "But those Woulda-Coulda-Shouldas all ran away and hid from one little Did."
>
> —*Shel Silverstein*

PART THREE: " . . . EVERYTHING ELSE WILL BE EASIER OR UNNECESSARY?"

Archimedes said, "Give me a lever long enough and I could move the world," and that's exactly what this last part tells you to find. "Everything else will be easier or unnecessary" is the ultimate leverage test. It tells you when you've found the first domino. It says that when you do this ONE Thing, everything else you could do to accomplish your goal will now be either doable with less effort or no longer even necessary. Most people struggle to comprehend how many things don't need to be done, if they would just start by doing the right thing. In effect, this qualifier seeks to declutter your life by asking you to put on blinders. This elevates the answer's potential to change your life by doing the leveraged thing and avoiding distractions.

The Focusing Question asks you to find the first domino and focus on it exclusively until you knock it over. Once you've done that, you'll discover a line of dominoes behind it either ready to fall or already down.

BIG IDEAS

1. **Great questions are the path to great answers.** The Focusing Question is a great question designed to find a great answer. It will help you find the first domino for your job, your business, or any other area in which you want to achieve extraordinary results.

2. **The Focusing Question is a double-duty question.** It comes in two forms: big picture and small focus. One is about finding the right direction in life and the other is about finding the right action.

3. **The Big-Picture Question: "What's my ONE Thing?"** Use it to develop a vision for your life and the direction for your career or company; it is your strategic compass. It also works when considering what you want to master, what you want to give to others and your community, and how you want to be remembered. It keeps your relationships with friends, family, and colleagues in perspective and your daily actions on track.

4. **The Small-Focus Question: "What's my ONE Thing right now?"** Use this when you first wake up and throughout the day. It keeps you focused on your most important work and, whenever you need it, helps you find the "levered action" or first domino in any activity. The small-focus question prepares you for the most productive workweek possible. It's effective in your personal life too, keeping you attentive to your most important immediate needs, as well as those of the most important people in your life.

Extraordinary results come from asking the Focusing Question. It's how you'll plot your course through life and business, and how you'll make the best progress on your most important work.

Whether you seek answers big or small, asking the Focusing Question is the ultimate success habit for your life.

11 THE SUCCESS HABIT

"Success is simple.
Do what's right,
the right way, at
the right time."

—Arnold H. Glasow

You know about habits. They can be hard to break—and hard to create. But we are unknowingly acquiring new ones all the time. When we start and continue a way of thinking or a way of acting over a long enough period, we've created a new habit. The choice we face is whether or not we want to form habits that get us what we want from life. If we do, then the Focusing Question is the most powerful success habit we can have.

For me, the Focusing Question is a way of life. I use it to find my most leveraged priority, make the most out of my time, and get the biggest bang for my buck. Whenever the outcome absolutely matters, I ask it. I ask it when I wake up and start my day. I ask it when I get to work, and again when I get home. *What's the ONE Thing I can do such that by doing it everything else will be easier or unnecessary?* And when I know the answer, I continue to ask it until I can see the connections and all my dominoes are lined up.

Obviously, you can drive yourself nuts analyzing every little aspect of everything you might do. I don't do that, and you shouldn't either. Start with the big stuff and see where it takes you. Over time, you'll develop your own sense of when to use the big-picture question and when to use the small-focus question.

The Focusing Question is the foundational habit I use to achieve extraordinary results and lead a big life. I use it for some things and not at all for others. I apply it to the important areas of my life: my spiritual life, physical health, personal life, key relationships, job, business, and financial life. And I address them in that order—each one is a foundation for the next.

Because I want my life to matter, I approach each area by doing what matters most in it. I view these as the cornerstones of my life and have found that when I'm doing what's most important in each area, my life feels like it's running on all cylinders.

The Focusing Question can direct you to your ONE Thing in the different areas of your life. Simply reframe the Focusing Question by inserting your area of focus. You can also include

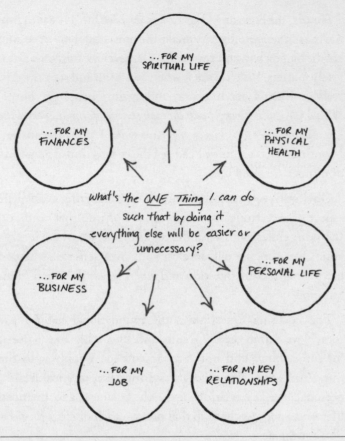

FIG. 16 My life and the areas that matter most in it.

a time frame—such as "right now" or "this year"—to give your answer the appropriate level of immediacy, or "in five years" or "someday" to find a big-picture answer that points you at outcomes to aim for.

Here are some Focusing Questions to ask yourself. Say the category first, then state the question, add a time frame, and end by adding "such that by doing it everything else will be easier or unnecessary?" For example: "*For my job,* what's the ONE Thing I can do to ensure I hit my goals *this week* such that by doing it everything else will be easier or unnecessary?"

FOR MY SPIRITUAL LIFE . . .

- What's the ONE Thing I can do to help others . . . ?
- What's the ONE Thing I can do to improve my relationship with God . . . ?

FOR MY PHYSICAL HEALTH . . .

- What's the ONE Thing I can do to achieve my diet goals . . . ?
- What's the ONE Thing I can do to ensure that I exercise . . . ?
- What's the ONE Thing I can do to relieve my stress . . . ?

FOR MY PERSONAL LIFE . . .

- What's the ONE Thing I can do to improve my skill at _____ . . . ?
- What's the ONE Thing I can do to find time for myself . . . ?

FOR MY KEY RELATIONSHIPS . . .

- What's the ONE Thing I can do to improve my relationship with my spouse/partner . . . ?
- What's the ONE Thing I can do to improve my children's school performance . . . ?
- What's the ONE Thing I can do to show my appreciation to my parents . . . ?

- What's the ONE Thing I can do to make my family stronger . . . ?

FOR MY JOB . . .

- What's the ONE Thing I can do to ensure that I hit my goals . . . ?
- What's the ONE Thing I can do to improve my skills . . . ?
- What's the ONE Thing I can do to help my team succeed . . . ?
- What's the ONE Thing I can do to further my career . . . ?

FOR MY BUSINESS . . .

- What's the ONE Thing I can do to make us more competitive . . . ?
- What's the ONE Thing I can do to make our product the best . . . ?
- What's the ONE Thing I can do to make us more profitable . . . ?
- What's the ONE Thing I can do to improve our customer experience . . . ?

FOR MY FINANCES . . .

- What's the ONE Thing I can do to increase my net worth . . . ?
- What's the ONE Thing I can do to improve my investment cash flow . . . ?
- What's the ONE Thing I can do to eliminate my credit card debt . . . ?

BIG IDEAS

So how do your make The ONE Thing part of your daily routine? How do you make it strong enough to get extraordinary results at work and in the other areas of your life? Here's a starter list drawn from our experience and our work with others.

1. **Understand and believe it.** The first step is to understand the concept of the ONE Thing, then to believe that it can make a difference in your life. If you don't understand and believe, you won't take action.

2. **Use it.** Ask yourself the Focusing Question. Start each day by asking, *"What's the ONE Thing I can do today for [whatever you want] such that by doing it everything else will be easier or even unnecessary?"* When you do this, your direction will become clear. Your work will be more productive and your personal life more rewarding.

3. **Make it a habit.** When you make asking the Focusing Question a habit, you fully engage its power to get the extraordinary results you want. It's a difference maker. Research says this will take about 66 days. Whether it takes you a few weeks or a few months, stick with it until it becomes your routine. If you're not serious about learning the Success Habit, you're not serious about getting extraordinary results.

4. **Leverage reminders.** Set up ways to remind yourself to use the Focusing Question. One of the best ways to do this is to put up a sign at work that says, "Until my ONE Thing is done—everything else is a distraction." We designed the back cover of this book to be a trigger —set it on the corner of your desk so that it's the

first thing you see when you get to work. Use notes, screen savers, and calendar cues to keep making the connection between the Success Habit and the results you seek. Put up reminders like, "The ONE Thing = Extraordinary Results" or "The Success Habit Will Get Me to My Goal."

5. **Recruit support.** Research shows that those around you can influence you tremendously. Starting a success support group with some of your work colleagues can help inspire all of you to practice the Success Habit every day. Get your family involved. Share your ONE Thing. Get them on board. Use the Focusing Question around them to show them how the Success Habit can make a difference in their school work, their personal achievements, or any other part of their lives.

This one habit can become the foundation for many more, so keep your Success Habit working as powerfully as possible. Use the strategies outlined in Part 3: Extraordinary Results, for goal setting and time blocking to experience extraordinary results every day of your life.

THE PATH TO
GREAT ANSWERS 12

The Focusing Question helps you identify your ONE Thing in any situation. It will clarify what you want in the big areas of your life and then drill down to what you must do to get them. It's really a simple process: You ask a great question, then you seek out a great answer. As simple as two steps, it's the ultimate Success Habit.

"People do not decide their futures, they decide their habits and their habits decide their futures."

—F. M. Alexander

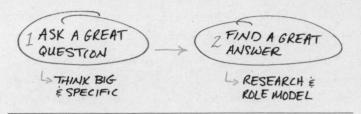

FIG. 17 Your one-two punch for extraordinary results.

1. ASK A GREAT QUESTION

The Focusing Question helps you ask a great question. Great questions, like great goals, are big and specific. They push you, stretch you, and aim you at big, specific answers. And because they're framed to be measurable, there's no wiggle room about what the results will look like.

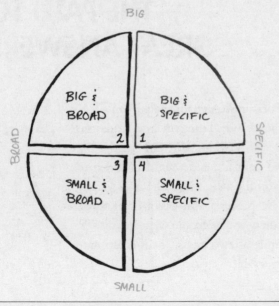

FIG. 18 Four options for framing a Great Question.

Look at the "Great Question" matrix (figure 18) to see the power of the Focusing Question.

Let's take increasing sales as a way to break down each of the quadrants, using "What can I do to double sales in six months?" as a placeholder for Big & Specific (figure 19).

Now, let's examine the pros and cons of each question quadrant, ending with where you want to be—Big & Specific.

Quadrant 4. Small & Specific: "What can I do to increase sales by 5 percent this year?" This aims you in a specific direction, but there's nothing truly challenging about this question. For most salespeople, a 5 percent bump in sales could just as easily happen because the market shifted in your favor rather than anything you might have done. At best it's

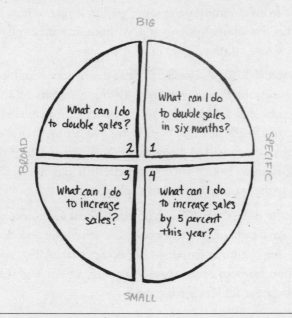

FIG. 19 Four options for framing a Great Question illustrated.

an incremental gain, not a life-changing leap forward. Low goals don't require extraordinary actions so they rarely lead to extraordinary results.

Quadrant 3. Small & Broad: "What can I do to increase sales?" This is not really an achievement question at all. It's more of a brainstorming question. It's great for listing your options but requires more to narrow your options and go small. How much will sales increase? By what date? Unfortunately, this is the kind of average question most people ask and then wonder why their answers don't deliver extraordinary results.

Quadrant 2. Big & Broad: "What can I do to double sales?" Here you have a big question, but nothing specific. It's a good start, but the lack of specifics leaves more questions than answers. Doubling sales in the next 20 years is very different from attempting the same goal in a year or less. There are still too many options and without specifics you won't know where to start.

Quadrant 1. Big & Specific: "What can I do to double sales in six months?" Now you have all the elements of a Great Question. It's a big goal and it's specific. You're doubling sales, and that's not easy. You also have a time frame of six months, which will be a challenge. You'll need a big answer. You'll have to stretch what you believe is possible and look outside the standard toolbox of solutions.

See the difference? When you ask a Great Question, you're in essence pursuing a great goal. And whenever you do this, you'll see the same pattern—Big & Specific. A big, specific question leads to a big, specific answer, which is absolutely necessary for achieving a big goal.

So if "What can I do to double sales in six months?" is a Great Question, how do you make it more powerful? Convert it to the Focusing Question: *"What's the ONE Thing I can do to double sales in six months such that by doing it everything else will be easier or unnecessary?"* Turning it into the Focusing Question goes to the heart of success by forcing you to identify what absolutely matters most and start there. Why?

Because that's where big success starts too.

2. FIND A GREAT ANSWER

The challenge of asking a Great Question is that, once you've asked it, you're now faced with finding a Great Answer.

Answers come in three categories: doable, stretch, and possibility. The easiest answer you can seek is the one that's already within reach of your knowledge, skills, and experience. With this type of solution you probably already know how to do it and won't have to change much to get it. Think of this as "doable" and the most likely to be achieved.

The next level up is a "stretch" answer. While this is still within your reach, it can be at the farthest end of your range. You'll most likely have to do some research and study what others have done to come up with this answer. Doing it can be iffy since you might have to extend yourself to the very limits of your current abilities. Think of this as potentially achievable and probable, depending on your effort.

High achievers understand these first two routes but reject them. Unwilling to settle for ordinary when extraordinary is possible, they've asked a Great Question and want the very best answer.

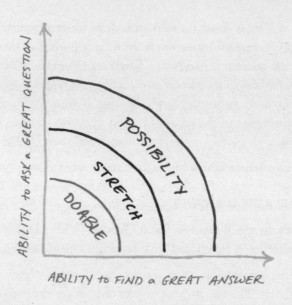

FIG. 20 The Success Habit unlocks possibilities.

Extraordinary results require a Great Answer.

Highly successful people choose to live at the outer limits of achievement. They not only dream of but deeply crave what is beyond their natural grasp. They know this type of answer is the hardest to come by, but also know that just by extending themselves to find it, they expand and enrich their life for the better.

If you want the most from your answer, you must realize that it lives outside your comfort zone. This is rare air. A big answer is never in plain view, nor is the path to finding one laid out for you. A possibility answer exists beyond what is already known and being done. As with a stretch goal, you can start out by doing research and studying the lives of other high achievers. But you can't stop there. In fact, your search has just begun. Whatever you learn, you'll use it to do what only the greatest achievers do: benchmark and trend.

A Great Answer is essentially a new answer. It is a leap across all current answers in search of the next one and is found in two steps. The first is the same as when you stretch. You uncover the best research and study the highest achievers. Anytime you don't know the answer, your answer is to go find your answer. In other words, by default, your first ONE Thing is to search for clues and role models to point you in the right direction. The first thing to do is ask, "Has anyone else studied or accomplished this or something like it?" The answer is almost always yes, so your investigation begins by finding out what others have learned.

One of the reasons I've amassed a large library of books over the years is because books are a great go-to resource. Short of having a conversation with someone who has accomplished what you hope to achieve, in my experience books and published works offer the most in terms of documented research and role models for success. The Internet has quickly become an invaluable tool as well. Whether offline or online, you're trying to find people who have already gone down the road you're traveling, so you can research, model, benchmark, and trend their experience. A college professor once told me, "Gary, you're smart, but people have lived before you. You're not the first person to dream big, so you'd be wise to study what others have learned first, and then build your actions on the back of their lessons." He was so right. And he was talking to you too.

The research and experience of others is the best place to start when looking for your answer. Armed with this

BENCHMARK

The benchmark is today's success—the trend is tomorrow's.

knowledge, you can establish a benchmark, the current high-water mark for all that is known and being done. With a stretch approach this was your maximum, but now it is your minimum. It's not all you'll do, but it becomes the hilltop where you'll stand to see if you can spot what might come next. This is called trending, and it's the second step. You're looking for the next thing you can do in the same direction that the best performers are heading or, if necessary, in an entirely new direction.

This is how big problems are solved and big challenges are overcome, for the best answers rarely come from an ordinary process. Whether it's figuring out how to leapfrog the competition, finding a cure for a disease, or coming up with an action step for a personal goal, benchmarking and trending is your best option. Because your answer will be original, you'll probably have to reinvent yourself in some way to implement it. A new answer usually requires new behavior, so don't be

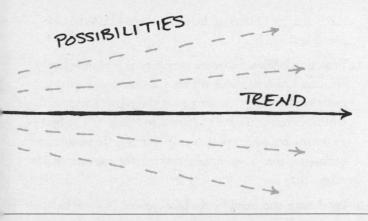

surprised if along the way to sizable success you change in the process. But don't let that stop you.

This is where the magic happens and possibilities are unlimited. As challenging as it can be, trailblazing up the path of possibilities is always worth it—for when we maximize our reach, we maximize our life.

(BIG IDEAS)

1. **Think big and specific.** Setting a goal you intend to achieve is like asking a question. It's a simple step from "I'd like to do that" to "How do I achieve that?" The best question—and by default, the best goal—is big and specific: big, because you're after extraordinary results; specific, to give you something to aim at and to leave no wiggle room about whether you hit the mark. A big and specific question, especially in the form of

the Focusing Question, helps you zero in on the best possible answer.

2. **Think possibilities.** Setting a doable goal is almost like creating a task to check off your list. A stretch goal is more challenging. It aims you at the edge of your current abilities; you have to stretch to reach it. The best goal explores what's possible. When you see people and businesses that have undergone transformations, this is where they live.

3. **Benchmark and trend for the best answer.** No one has a crystal ball, but with practice you can become surprisingly good at anticipating where things are heading. The people and businesses who get there first often enjoy the lion's share of the rewards with few, if any, competitors. Benchmark and trend to find the extraordinary answer you need for extraordinary results.

PART 3

EXTRAORDINARY RESULTS

UNLOCKING THE POSSIBILITIES WITHIN YOU

"Even if you're on the right
track, you'll get run over if
you just sit there."

—Will Rogers

EXTRAORDINARY RESULTS

There is a natural rhythm to our lives that becomes a simple formula for implementing the ONE Thing and achieving extraordinary results: purpose, priority, and productivity. Bound together, these three are forever connected and continually confirming each other's existence in our lives. Their link leads to the two areas where you'll apply the ONE Thing—one big and one small.

Your big ONE Thing is your purpose and your small ONE Thing is the priority you take action on to achieve it. The most productive people start with purpose and use it like a compass. They allow purpose to be the guiding force in determining the priority that drives their actions. This is the straightest path to extraordinary results.

Think of purpose, priority, and productivity as three parts of an iceberg.

With typically only 1/9 of an iceberg above water, whatever you see is just the tip of everything that is there. This is exactly how productivity, priority, and purpose are related. What you see is determined by what you don't.

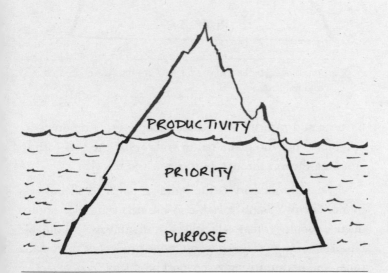

FIG. 22 Productivity is driven by purpose and priority.

The more productive people are, the more purpose and priority are pushing and driving them. With the additional outcome of profit, it's the same for business. What's visible to the public—productivity and profit—is always buoyed by the substance that serves as the company's foundation—

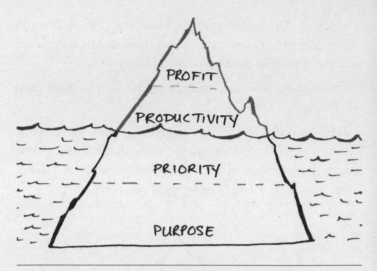

FIG. 23 In business, profit and productivity are also driven by priority and purpose.

purpose and priority. All businesspeople want productivity and profit, but too many fail to realize that the best path to attaining them is through purpose-driven priority.

Personal productivity is the building block of all business profit. The two are inseparable. A business can't have unproductive people yet magically still have an immensely profitable business. Great businesses are built one productive person at a time. And not surprisingly, the most productive people receive the greatest rewards from their businesses.

Connecting purpose, priority, and productivity determines how high above the rest successful individuals and profitable businesses rise. Understanding this is at the core of producing extraordinary results.

LIVE WITH PURPOSE 13

So, how do you use purpose to create an extraordinary life? Ebenezer Scrooge shows us how.

Cold-hearted, penny-pinching, and greedy, a man who despised Christmas and all things that give people happiness, his last name a byword for miserliness and meanness—Ebenezer Scrooge might have been the least likely candidate to teach us anything about how to live. Yet, in Charles Dickens's 1843 classic *A Christmas Carol*, he does.

> "Life isn't about finding yourself. Life is about creating yourself."
>
> —George Bernard Shaw

The redemptive tale of Scrooge's transformation from stingy, callous, and unloved to considerate, caring, and beloved is one of the best examples of how our destinies are determined by our decisions, our lives shaped by our choices. Once again, fiction provides us a formula we can all follow to build an extraordinary life with extraordinary results. I'd like to beg your forgiveness, take a little literary license, and quickly retell this timeless tale to show you.

One Christmas Eve, Ebenezer Scrooge is visited by the deceased spirit of Jacob Marley, his former business partner. We do not know if this is a dream or if it's real. Marley wails, "I am here tonight to warn you, that you have yet a chance and a hope of escaping my fate. You will be haunted by three spirits"—from the past, present, and future, as it turns out. "Remember what has passed between us!"

Now, let's stop for a second and bear in mind who Scrooge is. Dickens describes him as a man whose old features are frozen by the cold within him. Tight-fisted, with head down and hand to the grindstone, Scrooge pays as little as possible and keeps as much as he can. He is secretive and solitary. No one ever stops him in the streets to say hello. No one cares, for he cares for no one. He is a bitter, mean, covetous old sinner—cold to the sight, cold to the touch, and cold of heart, with no thaw in sight. His life is a lonely existence, and the world is worse off for it.

Over the course of the evening, the three spirits visit Scrooge to show him his past, present, and future. Through these visits he sees how he became the man he is, how his life is currently going, and what will ultimately happen to him and those around him. It's a terrifying experience that leaves him visibly shaken when he wakes the next morning. Not knowing whether it was real or a dream, but giddy upon discovering no time has passed, Scrooge realizes there is still time to alter his fate. In a joyous blur, he rushes into the street and instructs the first boy he sees to go buy the biggest turkey at the market and send it anonymously to the home of his sole employee, Bob Cratchit. Upon seeing a gentleman he'd once rebuffed for pleading charity for the needy, he prays for forgiveness and promises to donate huge sums of money to the poor.

Ebenezer eventually ends up at the home of his nephew, where he begs forgiveness for being such a fool for far too long and accepts an invitation to stay for holiday dinner. His nephew's wife and guests, shocked at his heartfelt bliss, can barely believe this is Scrooge.

The next morning, Bob Cratchit, upon arriving noticeably late to work, is confronted by Scrooge: "What do you mean coming here at this time of day? I am not going to stand for this sort of thing any longer!" Before this wretched news can sink in, the incredulous Cratchit hears him say, "And therefore I am about to raise your salary!"

Scrooge goes on to become the Cratchit family's benefactor. He finds a doctor for Tiny Tim, Cratchit's invalid son, and becomes like a second father to him. Scrooge lives out the rest of his days spending his time and money doing everything he can for others.

Through this simple story, Charles Dickens shows us a simple formula for creating an extraordinary life: Live with purpose. Live by priority. Live for productivity.

As I reflect on this story, I believe Dickens reveals purpose as a combination of where we're going and what's important to us. He implies that our priority is what we place the greatest importance on and our productivity comes from the actions we take. He lays out life as a series of connected choices, where our purpose sets our priority and our priority determines the productivity our actions produce.

To Dickens, our purpose determines who we are.

Scrooge is transparent and easy to understand, so let's revisit *A Christmas Carol* through the lens of Dickens's formula. At the place we enter his life, Scrooge's purpose is clearly about money. He pursues a life either working for it or being alone with it. He cares for money more than for people and believes that money is the end by which any means are justified. Based on his purpose, his priority is straightforward: making as much money for himself as he can. Collecting coin is what matters to Scrooge. As a result, his productivity is always aimed at making money. When he takes a break from making it, for fun, he counts it. Earning, netting, lending, receiving, tallying—these are the actions that fill his days, for he is greedy, selfish, and unmoved by the human condition of those around him.

By Scrooge's own standards, he's highly productive in accomplishing his purpose. By anyone else's, it's simply a miserable life.

This would be the end of the story, were it not for the perspective provided to Ebenezer by his former partner. Jacob Marley didn't want Scrooge to reach the same dead end he had. So, after the haunting, what happened to Scrooge? By Dickens's account, his purpose changed, which changed his most important priority, which changed where he focused his productivity. After Marley's intervention, Scrooge experienced the transformative power of a new purpose.

So, who did he become? Well, let's look.

As the narrative ends, Scrooge's purpose is no longer money, but people. He now cares about people. He cares about their financial circumstances and their physical condition. He sees himself happily in relationships with others, lending a hand any way he can. He values helping people more than hoarding money and believes money is good for the good it can do.

What is his priority? Where he once saved money and used people, he now uses money to save people. His overriding priority is to make as much money as he can so he can help as many as he can. His actions? He is productive throughout his days putting every penny he can toward others.

The transformation is remarkable, the message unmistakable. Who we are and where we want to go determine what we do and what we accomplish.

A life lived on purpose is the most powerful of all—and the happiest.

HAPPINESS ON PURPOSE

Ask enough people what they want in life and you'll hear happiness as the overwhelming response. Although we all have a wide variety of specific answers, happiness is what we most want—yet, it's what most of us understand the least. No matter our motivations, most of what we do in life is ultimately meant to make us happy. And yet we get it wrong. Happiness doesn't happen the way we think.

To explain, I want to share an ancient tale with you.

Upon coming out of his palace one morning and encountering a beggar, a king asks, "What do you want?" The beggar laughingly says, "You ask as though you can fulfill my desire!" Offended, the king replies, "Of course I can. What is it?" The beggar warns, "Think twice before you promise anything."

Now, the beggar was no ordinary beggar but the king's past-life master, who had promised in their former life, "I will come to try and wake you in our next life. This life you have missed, but I will come again to help you."

The king, not recognizing his old friend, insisted, "I will fulfill anything you ask, for I am a very powerful king who can fulfill any desire." The beggar said, "It is a very simple desire. Can you fill this begging bowl?" "Of course!" said the king, and he instructed his vizier to "fill the man's begging bowl with money." The vizier did, but when the money was poured into the bowl, it disappeared. So he poured more and more, but the moment he did, it would disappear.

The begging bowl remained empty.

Word spread throughout the kingdom, and a huge crowd gathered. The prestige and power of the king were at stake, so he told his vizier, "If my kingdom is to be lost, I am ready to lose it, but I cannot be defeated by this beggar." He continued to empty his wealth into the bowl. Diamonds, pearls, emeralds. His treasury was becoming empty.

And yet the begging bowl seemed bottomless. Everything put into it immediately disappeared!

Finally, as the crowd stood in utter silence, the king dropped at the beggar's feet and admitted defeat. "You are victorious, but before you go, fulfill my curiosity. What is the secret of this begging bowl?"

The beggar humbly replied, "There is no secret. It is simply made up of human desire."

One of our biggest challenges is making sure our life's purpose doesn't become a beggar's bowl, a bottomless pit of desire continually searching for the next thing that will make us happy. That's a losing proposition.

Acquiring money and obtaining things are pretty much all done for the pleasure we expect them to bring. On one hand, this actually works. Securing money or something we want can spike our happiness meter—for a moment. Then it goes back down. Over the ages, our greatest minds have pondered happiness, and their conclusions are much the same: having money and things won't automatically lead to lasting happiness.

How circumstances affect us depends on how we interpret them as they relate to our life. If we lack a "big picture" view, we can easily fall into serial success seeking. Why? Once we get what we want, our happiness sooner or later wanes because we quickly become accustomed to what we acquire. This happens to everyone and eventually leaves us bored, seeking something new to get or do. Worse, we may not even stop or slow down to enjoy what we've got because we automatically get up and go for something else. If we're not careful, we wind up ricocheting from achieving and acquiring to acquiring and achieving without ever taking time to fully enjoy any of it. This is a good way to remain a beggar, and the day we realize this is the day our life changes forever. So how do we find enduring happiness?

Happiness happens on the way to fulfillment.

Dr. Martin Seligman, past president of the American Psychological Association, believes there are five factors that contribute to our happiness: positive emotion and pleasure, achievement, relationships, engagement, and meaning. Of these, he believes engagement and meaning are the most important. Becoming more engaged in what we do by finding ways to make our life more meaningful is the surest way to finding lasting happiness. When our daily actions fulfill a bigger purpose, the most powerful and enduring happiness can happen.

Take money, for instance. Since money represents both getting something and the potential to get more, it makes for a great example. Many people not only misunderstand how to make money but also how it makes us happy. I've taught wealth building to everyone from seasoned entrepreneurs to high school students, and whenever I ask, "How much money do you want to earn?" I get all kinds of answers, but usually the number is quite high. When I ask, "How did you pick this number?" I frequently get the familiar answer: "Don't know." I then ask, "Can you tell me your definition of a financially wealthy person?" Invariably, I get numbers that start at a million dollars and go up from there. When I ask how they arrived at this, they often say, "It sounds like a lot." My response is, "It is, and it isn't. It all depends on what you'd do with it."

I believe that financially wealthy people are those who have enough money coming in without having to work to finance their purpose in life. Now, please realize that this definition presents a challenge to anyone who accepts it. To be financially wealthy you must have a purpose for your life. In other words, without purpose, you'll never know when you have enough money, and you can never be financially wealthy.

It isn't that having more money won't make you happy. To a point, it certainly can. But then it stops. For more money to continue to motivate you will depend on why you want more. It's been said that the end shouldn't justify the means, but be careful—when achieving happiness, any end you seek will only create happiness for you through the means it takes to achieve it. Wanting more money just for the sake of getting it won't bring the happiness you seek from it. Happiness happens when you have a bigger purpose than having more fulfills, which is why we say happiness happens on the way to fulfillment.

THE POWER OF PURPOSE

Purpose is the straightest path to power and the ultimate source of personal strength—strength of conviction and strength to persevere. The prescription for extraordinary results is knowing what matters to you and taking daily doses of actions in alignment with it. When you have a definite purpose for your life, clarity comes faster, which leads to more conviction in your direction, which usually leads to faster decisions. When you make faster decisions, you'll often be the one who makes the first decisions and winds up with the best choices. And when you have the best choices, you have the opportunity for the best experiences. This is how knowing where you're going helps lead you to the best possible outcomes and experiences life has to offer.

Purpose also helps you when things don't go your way. Life gets tough at times and there's no way around that. Aim high enough, live long enough, and you'll encounter your share of tough times. That's okay. We all experience this. Knowing why you're doing something provides the inspiration and motivation to give the extra perspiration needed to persevere when things go south. Sticking with something long enough for success to show up is a fundamental requirement for achieving extra-ordinary results.

Purpose provides the ultimate glue that can help you stick to the path you've set. When what you do matches your purpose, your life just feels in rhythm, and the path you beat with your feet seems to match the sound in your head and heart. Live with purpose and don't be surprised if you actually hum more and even whistle while you work.

When you ask yourself, "What's the ONE Thing I can do in my life that would mean the most to me and the world, such that by doing it everything else would be easier or unnecessary?" you're using the power of The ONE Thing to bring purpose to your life.

BIG IDEAS

1. **Happiness happens on the way to fulfillment.** We all want to be happy, but seeking it isn't the best way to find it. The surest path to achieving lasting happiness happens when you make your life about something bigger, when you bring meaning and purpose to your everyday actions.

2. **Discover your Big Why.** Discover your purpose by asking yourself what drives you. What's the thing that gets you up in the morning and keeps you going when you're

tired and worn down? I sometimes refer to this as your "Big Why." It's why you're excited with your life. It's why you're doing what you're doing.

3. **Absent an answer, pick a direction.** "Purpose" may sound heavy, but it doesn't have to be. Think of it as simply the ONE Thing you want your life to be about more than any other. Try writing down something you'd like to accomplish and then describe how you'd do it.

For me, it looks like this: "My purpose is to help people live their greatest life possible through my teaching, coaching, and writing." So, then what does my life look like?

Teaching is my ONE Thing and has been for almost 30 years. At first it was teaching clients about the market and how to make great decisions. Next, it was teaching salespeople in the classroom, during sales meetings, and one-on-one. Later it was teaching business classes. Then it became teaching high performers models and strategies for high achievement, and the last ten years it has been teaching seminars on specific life-building principles. What I teach is what I then coach and is supported by what I write.

Pick a direction, start marching down that path, and see how you like it. Time brings clarity, and if you find you don't like it, you can always change your mind. It's your life.

14 LIVE BY PRIORITY

"Planning is bringing
the future into the
present so that you
can do something
about it now."

—Alan Lakein

"Would you tell me, please, which way I ought to go from here?"

"That depends a good deal on where you want to get to," said the Cat.

"I don't much care where—" said Alice.

"Then it doesn't matter which way you go," said the Cat.

Alice's classic encounter with the Cheshire Cat in Lewis Carroll's *Alice's Adventures in Wonderland* reveals the close connection between purpose and priority. Live with purpose and you know where you want to go. Live by priority and you'll know what to do to get there.

When each day begins, we each have a choice. We can ask, "What shall I do?" or "What should I do?" Without direction, without purpose, whatever you "shall do" will always get you somewhere. But when you're going somewhere on purpose, there will always be something you "should do" that will get you where you *must* go. When your life is on purpose, living by priority takes precedence.

GOAL SETTING TO THE NOW

As Ebenezer Scrooge profoundly discovered, our life is driven by the purpose we give it. But there's a catch even he had to confront. Purpose has the power to shape our lives only in direct proportion to the power of the priority we connect it to. Purpose without priority is powerless.

To be precise, the word is *priority*—not priorities—and it originated in the 14th century from the Latin *prior*, meaning "first." If something *mattered the most* it was a "priority." Curiously, priority remained unpluralized until around the 20th century, when the world apparently demoted it to mean generally "something that matters" and the plural "priorities" appeared. With the loss of its initial intent, a wide variety of sayings like "most pressing matter," "prime concern," and "on the front burner" pitched in to recapture the essence of the original. Today, we elevate priority to its former meaning by adding "highest," "top," "first," "main," and "most important" in front of it. It would seem priority has traveled an interesting road.

So, watch your language. You may have many ways to talk about priority, but no matter the words you choose, to achieve extraordinary results your meaning must be the same—ONE Thing.

Whenever I teach goal setting I make it my top priority to show how a goal and a priority work together. I do this by asking, "Why do we set goals and create plans?" In spite of all the good answers I get, the truth is we have goals and plans for only one reason—to be appropriate in the moments of our lives that matter. While we may pull from the past and forecast the future, our only reality is the present moment. Right NOW is all we have to work with. Our past is but a former now, our future a potential one. To drive this point home, I started referring to the way to create a powerful priority as "Goal Setting to the Now" to emphasize why we were creating a priority in the first place.

The truth about success is that our ability to achieve extraordinary results in the future lies in stringing together powerful moments, one after the other. What you do in any given moment determines what you experience in the next. Your "present now" and all "future nows" are undeniably determined by the priority you live in the moment. The deciding factor in determining how you set that priority is who wins the battle between your present and future selves.

If you're offered a choice of $100 today or $200 next year, which would you choose? The $200, right? You would if your goal were to make the most money from the opportunity. Strangely, most people don't make that choice.

Economists have long known that even though people prefer big rewards over small ones, they have an even stronger preference for *present* rewards over *future* ones—even when the future rewards are MUCH BIGGER. It's an ordinary occurrence, oddly named *hyperbolic discounting*—the farther away a reward is in the future, the smaller the immediate motivation to achieve it. Maybe it's because objects that are farther away appear smaller, so people mistakenly assume they really are and discount their value. That might explain why so many people would actually choose the $100 today over twice the amount in the future. Their "present bias" overrides logic, and they allow a big future with potentially extraordinary results to get away. Now imagine the devastating impact living this way every day could have on your future self. Remember our conversation on delayed gratification? Turns out that what starts out as marshmallows can later cost you much more.

We need a simple way of thinking to save us from ourselves, set the right priority, and move closer toward accomplishing our purpose.

Goal Setting to the Now will get you there.

By thinking through the filter of Goal Setting to the Now, you set a future goal and then methodically drill down to what you should be doing right now. It can be a little like a Russian matryoshka doll in that your ONE Thing "right now" is nested inside your ONE Thing today, which is nested inside your ONE Thing this week, which is nested inside your ONE Thing this month. . . . It's how a small thing can actually build up to a big one.

You're lining up your dominoes.

GOAL SETTING to the NOW

SOMEDAY GOAL
What's the ONE Thing I want to do someday?
↓
FIVE-YEAR GOAL
Based on my Someday Goal,
what's the ONE Thing I can do in the next five years?
↓
ONE-YEAR GOAL
Based on my Five-Year Goal,
what's the ONE Thing I can do this year?
↓
MONTHLY GOAL
Based on my One-Year Goal,
what's the ONE Thing I can do this month?

↓
WEEKLY GOAL
Based on my Monthly Goal,
what's the ONE Thing I can do this week?
↓
DAILY GOAL
Based on my Weekly Goal,
what's the ONE Thing I can do today?
↓
RIGHT NOW
Based on my Daily Goal,
what's the ONE Thing I can do right now?

FIG. 24   Future purpose connects to present priority.

To understand how Goal Setting to the Now will guide your thinking and determine your most important priority, read this out loud to yourself:

> Based on my someday goal, what's the ONE Thing I can do in the next five years to be on track to achieve it? Now, based on my five-year goal, what's the ONE Thing I can do this year to be on track to achieve my five-year goal, so that I'm on track to achieve my someday goal? Now, based on my goal this year, what's the ONE Thing I can do this month so I'm on track to achieve my goal this year, so I'm on track to achieve my five-year goal, so I'm on track to achieve my someday goal? Now, based on my goal this month, what's the ONE Thing I can do this week so I'm on track to achieve my goal this month, so I'm on track to achieve my goal this year, so I'm on track to achieve my five-year goal, so I'm on track to achieve my someday goal? Now, based on my goal this week, what's the ONE Thing I can do today so I'm on track to achieve my goal this week, so I'm on track to achieve my goal this month, so I'm on track to achieve my goal this year, so I'm on track to achieve my five-year goal, so I'm on track to achieve my someday goal? So, based on my goal today, what's the ONE Thing I can do right NOW so I'm on track to achieve my goal today, so I'm on track to achieve my goal this week, so I'm on track to achieve my goal this month, so I'm on track to achieve my goal this year, so I'm on track to achieve my five-year goal, so I'm on track to achieve my someday goal?

I hope you hung in there and read the entire thing. Why? Because you're training your mind how to think, how to connect one goal with the next over time until you know the most important thing you must do right NOW. You're learning how to think big—but go small.

To prove its value, just skip the steps by asking yourself, "What's the ONE Thing I can do right now so I'm on track to achieve my someday goal?" Doesn't work. The moment is too far from the future for you to clearly see your key priority. In fact, you can keep adding back in today, this week, and so on, but you won't see the powerful priority you seek until you've added back in all the steps. It's why most people never get close to their goals. They haven't connected today to all the tomorrows it will take to get there.

Connect today to all your tomorrows. It matters.

Research backs this up. In three separate studies, psychologists observed 262 students to see the impact of visualization on outcomes. The students were asked to visualize in one of two ways: Those in one group were told to visualize the *outcome* (like getting an "A" on an exam) and the others were asked to visualize the *process* needed to achieve a desired outcome (like all of the study sessions needed to earn that "A" on the exam). In the end, students who visualized the process performed better across the board—they studied earlier and more frequently and earned higher grades than those who simply visualized the outcome.

People tend to be overly optimistic about what they can accomplish, and therefore most don't think things all the way through. Researchers call this the "planning fallacy." Visualizing the process—breaking a big goal down into the steps needed to achieve it—helps engage the strategic thinking you need to plan for and achieve extraordinary results. This is why Goal Setting to the Now really works.

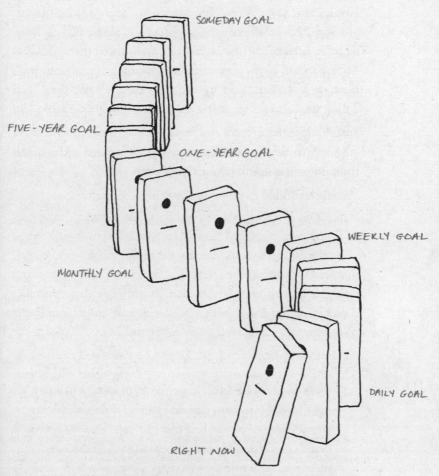

WHAT'S MY ONE THING?

SOMEDAY GOAL

FIVE-YEAR GOAL

ONE-YEAR GOAL

WEEKLY GOAL

MONTHLY GOAL

DAILY GOAL

RIGHT NOW

WHAT'S MY ONE THING
RIGHT NOW?

FIG. 25 Living a domino run.

I have this dialogue with people every day. It's particularly effective when they ask me what they should do. I turn it around and say, "Before I answer your question, let me ask you something: Where are you going, and where do you want to be someday?" Without fail, as I walk them through Goal Setting to the Now, they catch on quickly and come up with their own answers, and by the time they tell me the ONE Thing they should be doing right now, I laughingly ask, "So why are you still talking to me?"

Your last step is to write down your answers. Much has been written about writing down goals and for a very good reason—it works.

In 2008, Dr. Gail Matthews of the Dominican University of California, recruited 267 participants from a wide range of professions (lawyers, accountants, nonprofit employees, marketers, etc.) and a variety of countries. Those who wrote down their goals were 39.5 percent more likely to accomplish them. Writing down your goals and your most important priority is your final step to living by priority.

BIG IDEAS

1. **There can only be ONE.** Your most important priority is the ONE Thing you can do right now that will help you achieve what matters most to you. You may have many "priorities," but dig deep and you'll discover there is always one that matters most, your top priority—your ONE Thing.

2. **Goal Set to the Now.** Knowing your future goal is how you begin. Identifying the steps you need to

accomplish along the way keeps your thinking clear while you uncover the right priority you need to accomplish right now.

3. **Put pen to paper.** Write your goals down and keep them close.

Pull your purpose through to a single priority built by Goal Setting to the Now, and that priority—that ONE Thing you can do such that by doing it everything else will be easier or unnecessary—will show you the way to extraordinary results.

And once you know what to do, the only thing left is to go from knowing to doing.

15 LIVE FOR PRODUCTIVITY

"Productivity isn't about being a workhorse, keeping busy or burning the midnight oil. . . . It's more about priorities, planning, and fiercely protecting your time."

—Margarita Tartakovsky

Ebenezer Scrooge's story might have been a footnote in literary history except for this—he acted. Passionate about his new purpose and empowered by a priority that fulfilled it, he got up and got going.

Productive action transforms lives.

"Let's go be productive!" will never be heard in the movies as the cavalry takes the hill. It's not the first choice a coach, manager, or general uses as a rallying cry to arouse deep emotion and inspire the troops. It's not what you say to yourself as you take a deep breath and dive into a challenge or face competition. And Dickens never had Scrooge utter these words as he took command of his transformed life. Yet *productive* is exactly what Scrooge was, and there's no better word than *productivity* to describe what you want from what you do when the outcome matters.

We are always doing something—working, playing, eating, sleeping, standing, sitting, breathing. If we're alive, we're doing something. Even if we're doing nothing, that's something. Every minute of every day, the question is never will we be doing something, but rather what that something is we'll be doing. Sometimes what we do doesn't matter, but sometimes it does. And when it does, what we do defines our life more than anything else. In the end, putting together a life of extraordinary results simply comes down to getting the most out of what you do, when what you do matters.

Living for productivity produces extraordinary results.

Whenever I teach productivity I always start by asking, "What type of time-managing system do you use?" The answers are as varied as the number of people in the room: paper calendar, electronic calendar, Day-Timer, At-A-Glance weekly planner . . . you name it and I hear it. I then ask, "So how did you choose yours?" The reasons cited come in every shape, size, color, price, and criteria imaginable. But the students invariably describe the format, not the function—what they are, not how they work. So when I say, "That's great, but what kind of *system* do you use?" the answer is always the same: "What do you mean?"

"Well, if everyone has the same amount of time and yet some earn more than others," I ask, "can we then say that it's how we use our time that determines the money we make?" Everyone always agrees, so I continue: "If this is true, that time is money, then the best way to describe a time-managing system might just be by the money it makes. So, do you think you're using the $10,000-a-year system? The $20,000-a-year system? The $50,000-, $100,000-, or $500,000-a-year system? Are you using the $1,000,000-plus system?"

Silence.

Until inevitably someone asks, "How do we know?"

To which I reply, "How much do you make?"

If money is a metaphor for producing results, then it's clear—a time-managing system's success can be judged by the productivity it produces.

The strange thing about my life is that I've never worked for anyone who wasn't a millionaire or didn't become one. I didn't set out for this to happen. It just did. And the most important thing I learned from these experiences is that the most successful people are the most productive people.

Productive people get more done, achieve better results, and earn far more in their hours than the rest. They do so because they devote maximum time to being productive on their top priority, their ONE Thing. They time block their ONE Thing and then protect their time blocks with a vengeance. They've connected the dots between working their time blocks consistently and the extra-ordinary results they seek.

> "My goal is no longer to get more done, but rather to have less to do."
>
> —Francine Jay

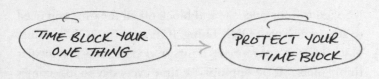

FIG. 26 Make an appointment with yourself and keep it!

TIME BLOCKING

I often say that I come from a "long line of lethargic people." This is usually good for a laugh, but it's also true. It seems at times that my genes just might have more in common with the tortoise than the hare. On the other hand, some of the people I work with are so blessed with energy they actually vibrate. Amazingly, they're able to work long hours over extended periods and never wear down. When I try to follow suit, in less than a week my body simply falls apart. I've discovered that, no matter how hard I try, I can't use more time as my main means of doing more. It's just not physically possible for me. So, given my constraints, I've had to find a way to be highly productive in the hours I *can* put in.

The solution? Time blocking.

Most people think there's never enough time to be successful, but there is when you block it. Time blocking is a very results-oriented way of viewing and using time. It's a way of making sure that what has to be done *gets* done. Alexander Graham Bell said, "Concentrate all your thoughts upon the work at hand. The sun's rays do not burn until brought to a focus." Time blocking harnesses your energy and centers it on your most important work. It's productivity's greatest power tool.

So, go to your calendar and block off all the time you need to accomplish your ONE Thing. If it's a onetime ONE Thing, block off the appropriate hours and days. If it's a regular thing, block off the appropriate time every day so it becomes a habit. Everything else—other projects, paperwork, e-mail, calls, correspondence, meetings, and all the other stuff— must wait. When you time block like this, you're creating the most productive day possible in a way that's repeatable every day for the rest of your life.

Unfortunately, if you're like most individuals, your typical day might look something like figure 27, when you find yourself with less and less time to focus on what matters most.

The most productive people's day is dramatically different (figure 28).

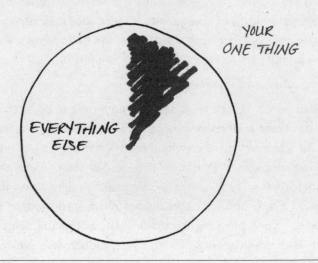

THE TYPICAL DAY

YOUR
ONE THING

EVERYTHING
ELSE

FIG. 27 Everything Else dominates your day!

If disproportionate results come from one activity, then you must give that one activity disproportionate time. Each and every day, ask this Focusing Question for your blocked time: *"Today, what's the ONE Thing I can do for my ONE Thing such that by doing it everything else will be easier or unnecessary?"* When you find the answer, you'll be doing the most leveraged activity for your most leveraged work.

This is how results become extraordinary.

Those who do this, in my experience, are the ones who not only become the most accomplished, but who also have the most career opportunities. Slowly but surely they become known in their organization for their ONE Thing and

THE PRODUCTIVE DAY

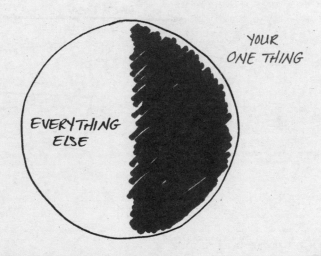

FIG. 28 Your ONE Thing gets the time of day it deserves!

become "irreplaceable." Ultimately, no one can imagine or tolerate the cost of losing them. (The opposite is equally true, by the way, for those lost in the land of "Everything Else.")

Once you've done your ONE Thing for the day, you can devote the rest of it to everything else. Just use the Focusing Question to identify your next priority and give that task the time it deserves. Repeat this approach until your workday is done. Getting "everything else" done may help you sleep better at night, but it's unlikely to earn you a promotion.

TIME BLOCKING

MON	TUE	WED	TH	FRI	SAT	SUN
1 YOUR ONE THING	2 YOUR ONE THING	3 YOUR ONE THING	4 YOUR ONE THING	5 YOUR ONE THING	6	7 PLAN
8 YOUR ONE THING	9 YOUR ONE THING	10 YOUR ONE THING	11	12	13	14
			← VACATION →			
15 YOUR ONE THING	16 YOUR ONE THING	17 YOUR ONE THING	18 YOUR ONE THING	19 YOUR ONE THING	20	21 PLAN
22 YOUR ONE THING	23 YOUR ONE THING	24 YOUR ONE THING	25 YOUR ONE THING	26 YOUR ONE THING	27	28 PLAN

FIG. 29 Your time-blocking calendar.

Time blocking works on the premise that a calendar records appointments but doesn't care who those appointments are with. So, when you know your ONE Thing, make an appointment with yourself to tackle it. Every day great salespeople generate leads, great programmers program, and great artists paint. Take any profession or any position and fill in the blank. Great success shows up when time is devoted every day to becoming great.

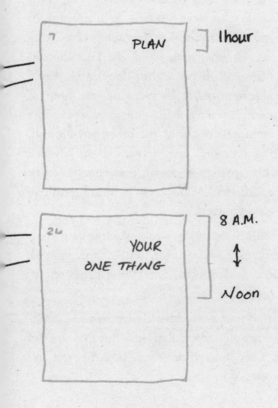

To achieve extraordinary results and experience greatness, time block these three things in the following order:

1. Time block your time off.
2. Time block your ONE Thing.
3. Time block your planning time.

1. TIME BLOCK YOUR TIME OFF

Extraordinarily successful people launch their year by taking time out to plan their time off. Why? They know they'll need it and they know they'll be able to afford it. In truth, the most successful simply see themselves as working between vacations. On the other hand, the least successful don't reserve time off, because they don't think they'll deserve it or be able to afford it. By planning your time off in advance, you are, in effect, managing your work time around your downtime instead of the other way around. You're also letting everyone else know well in advance when you'll be out so they can plan accordingly. When you intend to be successful, you start by protecting time to recharge and reward yourself.

Take time off. Block out long weekends and long vacations, then take them. You'll be more rested, more relaxed, and more productive afterward. Everything needs rest to function better, and you're no different.

Resting is as important as working. There are a few examples of successful people who violate this, but they are not our role models. They succeed in spite of how they rest and renew—not because of it.

2. TIME BLOCK YOUR ONE THING

After you've time blocked your time off, time block your ONE Thing. Yes, you read that right. Your most important work comes second. Why? Because you can't happily sustain success in your professional life if you neglect your personal "re-creation" time. Time block your time off, and then make time for your ONE Thing.

The most productive people, the ones who experience extraordinary results, design their days around doing their ONE Thing. Their most important appointment each day is with themselves, and they never miss it. If they complete their ONE Thing before their time block is done, they don't necessarily call it a day. They use the Focusing Question to tell them how they can use the time they have left.

Similarly, if they have a specific goal for their ONE Thing, they finish it, regardless of the time. In *A Geography of Time*, Robert Levine points out that most people work on "clock" time—*"It's five o'clock, I'll see you tomorrow"*—while others work on "event" time—*"My work is done when it's done."* Think about it. The dairy farmer doesn't get to knock off at any certain time; he goes home when the cows have been milked. It's the same for any position in any profession where results matter. The most productive people work on event time. They don't quit until their ONE Thing is done.

The key to making this work is to block time as early in your day as you possibly can. Give yourself 30 minutes

> "Day, n. A period of twenty-four hours, mostly misspent."
>
> —Ambrose Bierce

to an hour to take care of morning priorities, then move to your ONE Thing.

My recommendation is to block four hours a day. This isn't a typo. I repeat: *four hours* a day. Honestly, that's the minimum. If you can do more, then do it.

In *On Writing*, Stephen King describes his work flow: "My own schedule is pretty clear-cut. Mornings belong to whatever is new—the current composition. Afternoons are for naps and letters. Evenings are for reading, family, Red Sox games on TV, and any revisions that just cannot wait. Basically, mornings are my prime writing time." Four hours a day may scare you more than King's novels, but you can't argue with his results. Stephen King is one of the most successful and prolific writers of our time.

Whenever I tell this story, there is always one person who says to me, "Well, sure, it's easy for Stephen King—he's Stephen King!" To that I simply say, "I think the question you must ask yourself is this: Does he get to do this because he is Stephen King, or is he Stephen King because he does this?" That invariably stops that discussion cold.

Like so many other successful writers, early in his career King had to find his time blocks where he could—mornings, evenings, even lunch breaks—because his day job didn't accommodate his ambition for his life. Once extraordinary results started showing up and he could earn a living from his ONE Thing, he was able to move his time blocks to a more sustainable time.

An executive assistant on our team recently transitioned to blocking large chunks of time for a project. It was stressful at first. She was continually interrupted. E-mail alerts pinged, colleagues dropped by, team members provided a steady stream of requests for her time. These weren't even distractions—they were her job. In the end, she had to borrow a laptop and book a conference room to escape "drive-bys" and random, nonurgent requests. But within just a week, everyone became accustomed to the fact that for regular periods of time she would not be accessible. They adjusted. It took a week. Not a month or a year. *A week.* Meetings got rescheduled and life went on. And she experienced a huge leap in productivity.

> "Efficiency is doing the thing right. Effectiveness is doing the right thing."
>
> —Peter Drucker

No matter who you are, large time blocks work.

Paul Graham's 2009 essay "Maker's Schedule, Manager's Schedule" underscores the need for large time blocks. Graham, one of the founders of the innovative venture capital firm Y Combinator, argues that normal business culture gets in the way of the very productivity it seeks because of the way people traditionally schedule their time (or are allowed to).

Graham divides all work into two buckets: maker (do or create) and manager (oversee or direct). "Maker" time requires large blocks of the clock to write code, develop ideas, generate leads, recruit people, produce products, or execute on projects and plans. This time tends to be viewed in half-day increments. "Manager time," on the other hand, gets divided into hours. This time typically has one moving from meeting to meeting, and because those who oversee or direct tend to have power and authority, "they are in a position to make everyone resonate at their frequency." This can create a huge conflict if those needing maker time are pulled into meetings at odd hours, destroying the very time blocks they need to move themselves and the company forward. Graham embraced this insight and created a company culture at Y Combinator that now runs completely on a maker's schedule. All meetings get clustered at the end of the day.

To experience extraordinary results, be a maker in the morning and a manager in the afternoon. Your goal is "ONE and done." But if you don't time block each day to do your ONE Thing, your ONE Thing won't become a done thing.

3. TIME BLOCK YOUR PLANNING TIME

The last priority you time block is planning time. This is when you reflect on where you are and where you want to go. For annual planning, schedule this time late enough in the year that you have a sense of your trajectory, but not so late that you lose your running start for the next. Take a look at your someday and five-year goals and assess the progress you must make in the next year to be on track. You may even add new goals, re-envision old ones, or eliminate any that no longer reflect your purpose or priorities.

Block an hour each week to review your annual and monthly goals. First, ask what needs to happen that month for you to be on target for your annual goals. Then ask what must happen that week to be on course for your monthly goals. You're essentially asking, "Based on where I am right now, what's the ONE Thing I need to do this week to stay on track for my monthly goal and for my monthly goal to be on track for my annual goal?" You're lining up the dominoes. Decide how much time you'll need to achieve this, and reserve that amount of time on your calendar. In effect, you could say that when you time block your planning time, you're really time blocking your time to time block. Think about it.

In July 2007, software developer Brad Isaac shared a productivity secret he reportedly got from comedian Jerry Seinfeld. Before Seinfeld was a household name and still regularly toured, Isaac ran into him at an open-mike comedy club and asked him for advice on how to be a better comedian. Seinfeld told him the key was to write jokes (hint: his ONE Thing!) *every* day. And the way he'd figured out how to make that happen was to hang a huge annual calendar on the wall and then put a big red X across every day he

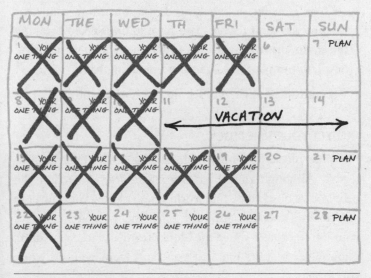

FIG. 30   X's add up to eXtraordinary results!

worked on his craft. "After a few days, you'll have a chain," Seinfeld said. "Just keep at it and the chain will grow longer every day. You'll like seeing the chain, especially when you get a few weeks under your belt. Your only job is to not break the chain. *Don't break the chain.*"

What I love about Seinfeld's method is that it resonates with everything I know to be true. It's simple. It's based on doing ONE Thing, and it creates its own momentum. You could look at the calendar and be overwhelmed: "How can I commit to this for an entire year?" But the system is designed to bring your biggest goal to the now and simply focus on making the next **X**. As Walter Elliot said, "Perseverance is not a long race; it is many short races one after another." As you complete these short races and get a chain going, it gets easier and easier. Momentum and motivation start to take over.

There is magic in knocking down your most important domino day after day. All you have to do is avoid breaking the chain, one day at a time, until you generate a powerful new habit in your life—the time-blocking habit.

Sound simple? Time blocking is—if you protect it.

PROTECT YOUR TIME BLOCK

For time blocks to actually block time, they must be protected. Although time blocking isn't hard, protecting the time you've blocked is. The world doesn't know your purpose or priorities and isn't responsible for them—you are. So it's your job to protect your time blocks from all those who don't know what matters most to you, and from yourself when you forget.

The best way to protect your time blocks is to adopt the mindset that they can't be moved. So, when someone tries to double-book you, just say, "I'm sorry, I already have an appointment at that time," and offer other options. If the other person is disappointed, you're sympathetic but ultimately unmoved. Extraordinarily results-oriented people—the very people who have the most demands on their time—do this every day. They keep their most important appointment.

The toughest part is navigating a high-level request. How do you say no to anyone important—your boss, a key client, your mom—who asks you to do something with a high sense of urgency? One way is to say yes and then ask, "If I have that done by [a specific time in the future], would that work?" Most often, these requests are more about an immediate need to hand a task off than about a need for it to be done immediately, so the requester usually just wants to know it *will* get done. Sometimes the request is real, needs to be done now, and you must drop what you're doing and do it. In this situation, follow the rule "If you erase, you must replace" and immediately reschedule your time block.

Then there's you. If you're already feeling overbooked and overworked, it can seem incredibly challenging to hold to a time block. It can be hard to imagine how everything else will get done when so much time is given to ONE Thing. The key is to fully internalize the domino fall that will happen when your ONE Thing gets done, and remember that everything else you might do or have to do will be easier or unnecessary. When I first began to time block, the most effective thing I did was to put up a sheet of paper that said, "Until My ONE Thing Is Done—Everything Else Is A Distraction!" Try it. Put it where you can see it and others can see it as well.

Then make this the mantra you say to yourself and everyone else. In time, others will begin to understand how you work and support it. Just watch.

The last thing that can knock you off your time block is when you can't free your mind. Day in and day out, your own need to do other things instead of your ONE Thing may be your biggest challenge to overcome. Life doesn't simplify itself the moment you simplify your focus; there's always other stuff screaming to be done. Always. So when stuff pops into your head, just write it down on a task list and get back to what you're supposed to be doing. In other words, do a brain dump. Then put it out of sight and out of mind until its time comes.

In the end, there are plenty of ways your time block can get sabotaged. Here are four proven ways to battle distractions and keep your eye on your ONE Thing.

1. **Build a bunker.** Find somewhere to work that takes you out of the path of disruption and interruption. If you have an office, get a "Do Not Disturb" sign. If it has glass walls, install shades. If you work in a cubicle, get permission to put up a folding screen. If necessary, go elsewhere. The immortal Ernest Hemingway kept a strict writing schedule starting at seven every morning in his bedroom. The mortal but still immensely talented business author Dan Heath "bought an old laptop, deleted all its browsers, and, for good measure, deleted its wireless network drivers" and would take his "way-back machine" to a coffee shop to avoid distractions. Between the two extremes, you could just find a vacant room and simply close the door.

2. **Store provisions.** Have any supplies, materials, snacks, or beverages you need on hand and, other than for a bathroom break, avoid leaving your bunker. A simple trip to the coffee machine can derail your day should you encounter someone seeking to make you a part of theirs.

3. **Sweep for mines.** Turn off your phone, shut down your e-mail, and exit your Internet browser. Your most important work deserves 100 percent of your attention.

4. **Enlist support.** Tell those most likely to seek you out what you're doing and when you'll be available. It's amazing how accommodating others are when they see the big picture and know when they can access you.

If, ultimately, you continue a tug-of-war to make time blocking take place, then use the Focusing Question to ask: *What's the ONE Thing I can do to protect my time block every day such by doing it everything else I might do will be easier or unnecessary?*

BIG IDEAS

1. **Connect the dots.** Extraordinary results become possible when where you want to go is completely aligned with what you do today. Tap into your purpose and allow that clarity to dictate your priorities. With your priorities clear, the only logical course is to go to work.

2. **Time block your ONE Thing.** The best way to make your ONE Thing happen is to make regular appointments with yourself. Block time early in the day, and block big chunks of it—no less than four hours! Think of it

this way: If your time blocking were on trial, would your calendar contain enough evidence to convict you?

3. **Protect your time block at all costs.** Time blocking works only when your mantra is "Nothing and no one has permission to distract me from my ONE Thing." Unfortunately, your resolve won't keep the world from trying, so be creative when you can be and firm when you must. Your time block is the most important meeting of your day, so whatever it takes to protect it is what you have to do.

The people who achieve extraordinary results don't achieve them by working more hours. They achieve them by getting more done in the hours they work.

Time blocking is one thing; productive time blocking is another.

THE THREE COMMITMENTS 16

Achieving extraordinary results through time blocking requires three commitments. First, you must adopt the mindset of someone seeking mastery. Mastery is a commitment to becoming your best, so to achieve extraordinary results you must embrace the extraordinary effort it represents. Second, you must continually seek the very best ways of doing things. Nothing is more futile than doing your best using an approach that can't deliver results equal to your effort. And last, you

"Nobody who ever gave his best regretted it."

—*George Halas*

must be willing to be held accountable to doing everything you can to achieve your ONE Thing. Live these commitments and you give yourself a fighting chance to experience extraordinary.

THE THREE COMMITMENTS TO YOUR ONE THING

1. Follow the Path of Mastery
2. Move from "E" to "P"
3. Live the Accountability Cycle

1. FOLLOW THE PATH OF MASTERY

Mastery isn't a word we often hear anymore, but it's as critical as ever to achieving extraordinary results. As intimidating as it might initially seem, when you can see mastery as a path you go down instead of a destination you arrive at, it starts to feel accessible and attainable. Most assume mastery is an end result, but at its core, mastery is a way of thinking, a way of acting, and a journey you experience. When what you've chosen to master is the right thing, then pursuing mastery of it will make everything else you do either easier or no longer necessary. That's why what you choose to master matters.

Mastery plays a key role in your domino run.

I believe the healthy view of mastery means giving the best you have to become the best you can be at your most important work. The path is one of an apprentice learning and relearning the basics on a never-ending journey of greater experience and expertise. Think of it this way: At some point white belts training to advance know the same basic karate moves black belts know—they simply haven't practiced enough to be able to do them as well. The creativity you see at a black-belt level comes from mastery of the white-belt fundamentals. Since there is always another level to learn, mastery actually means you're a master of what you know and an apprentice of what you don't. In other words, we become masters of what is behind us and apprentices for what is ahead. This is why mastery is a journey. Alex Van Halen has said that when he would go out at night his brother Eddie would be sitting on his bed practicing the guitar, and when he came home many hours later Eddie would be in the same place, still practicing. That's the journey of mastery—it never ends.

In 1993, psychologist K. Anders Ericsson published "The Role of Deliberate Practice in the Acquisition of Expert Performance" in the journal *Psychological Review*. As the benchmark for understanding mastery, this article debunked the idea that an expert performer was *gifted*, a *natural*, or even a *prodigy*. Ericsson essentially gave us our first real insights into mastery and birthed the idea of the "10,000-hour rule." His research identified a common pattern of regular and deliberate practice over the course of years in elite performers that made them what they were—elite. In one study, elite violinists had separated themselves from all others by each accumulating more than 10,000 hours of practice by age 20. Thus the rule. Many elite performers complete their journey in about ten years, which, if you do the math, is an average of about three hours of deliberate practice a day, every day, 365 days a year. Now, if your ONE Thing relates to work and you put in 250 workdays a year (five days a week for 50 weeks), to keep pace on your mastery journey you'll need to average four hours a day. Sound familiar? It's not a random number. That's the amount of time you need to time block every day for your ONE Thing.

More than anything else, expertise tracks with hours invested. Michelangelo once said, "If the people knew how hard I had to work to gain my mastery, it wouldn't seem wonderful at all." His point is obvious. Time on a task, over time, eventually beats talent every time. I'd say you can "book that," but actually you should "block it."

When you commit to time block your ONE Thing, make sure you approach it with a mastery mentality. This will give you the best opportunity to be the most productive you can be, and ultimately the best you can become. And here's what's interesting: the more productive you are, the more likely you are to receive several additional payoffs you would otherwise have missed. The pursuit of mastery bears gifts.

As you progress along the path of mastery, both your self-confidence and your success competence will grow. You'll make a discovery: the path of mastery is not so different from one pursuit to the next. What might pleasantly surprise you is how giving yourself over to mastering ONE Thing serves as a platform for, and speeds up the process of, doing other things. Knowledge begets knowledge and skills build on skills. It's what makes future dominoes fall more easily.

Mastery is a pursuit that keeps giving, because it's a path that never ends. In his landmark book *Mastery,* George Leonard tells the story of Jigoro Kano, the founder of judo. According to legend, as Kano approached death, he called his students around him and asked to be buried in his white belt. The symbolism wasn't lost. The highest-ranking martial artist of his discipline embraced the emblem of the beginner for his life and beyond, because to him the journey of the successful lifelong learner was never over. Time blocking is essential to mastery, and mastery is essential to time blocking. They go hand in hand—when you do one, you do the other.

2. MOVE FROM "E" TO "P"

When coaching top performers, I often ask, "Are you doing this to simply do the best you can do, or are you doing this to do it the best it can be done?" Although it's not meant to be a trick question, it trips people up anyway. Many realize that although they are giving their best effort, they aren't doing the best that could be done, because they aren't willing to change what they are doing. The path of mastering something is the combination of not only doing the best *you* can do at it, but also doing it the best *it* can be done. Continually improving how you do something is critical to getting the most from time blocking.

It's called moving from "E" to "P."

When we roll out of bed in the morning and start tackling the day, we do so in one of two ways: Entrepreneurial ("E") or Purposeful ("P"). Entrepreneurial is our natural approach. It's seeing something we want to do or that needs to be done and racing off to do it with enthusiasm, energy, and our natural abilities. No matter the task, all natural ability has a ceiling of achievement, a level of productivity and success that eventually tops out. Although this varies from person to person and task to task, everybody in life has a natural ceiling for everything. Give some people a hammer and they're an instant carpenter. Give one to me and I'm all thumbs. In other words, some people can naturally use a hammer extremely well with minimal instruction or practice, but there are others, like me, who hit their ceiling of achievement the moment they're holding one. If the outcome of your efforts is acceptable at whatever level of achievement you reach, then you high-five and move on. But when you're going about your ONE Thing, any ceiling of achievement must be challenged, and this requires a different approach— a Purposeful approach.

Highly productive people don't accept the limitations of their natural approach as the final word on their success. When they hit a ceiling of achievement, they look for new models and systems, better ways to do things to push them through. They pause just long enough to examine their options, they pick the best one, and then they're right back at it. Ask an "E" to cut some firewood and the Entrepreneurial person would likely shoulder an axe and head straight for the woods. On the other hand, the Purposeful person might ask, "Where can I get a chainsaw?" With a "P" mindset, you

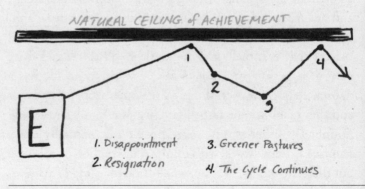

THE ENTREPRENEURIAL APPROACH

"Doing What Comes Naturally"

NATURAL CEILING of ACHIEVEMENT

E

1. Disappointment
2. Resignation
3. Greener Pastures
4. The Cycle Continues

FIG. 31 In the long run, "P" beats "E" every time.

can achieve breakthroughs and accomplish things far beyond your natural abilities. You must simply be willing to do whatever it takes.

You can't put limits on what you'll do. You have to be open to new ideas and new ways of doing things if you want breakthroughs in your life. As you travel the path of mastery you'll find yourself continually challenged to do new things. The Purposeful person follows the simple rule that "a different result requires doing something different." Make this your mantra and breakthroughs become possible.

Too many people reach a level where their performance is "good enough" and then stop working on getting better. People on the path to mastery avoid this by continually upping their goal, challenging themselves to break through

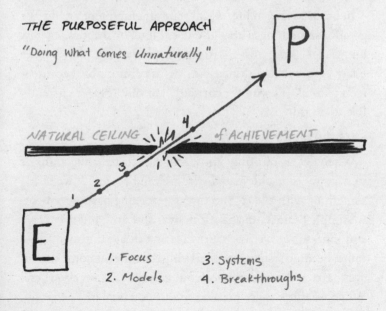

THE PURPOSEFUL APPROACH

"Doing What Comes Unnaturally"

NATURAL CEILING of ACHIEVEMENT

P

E

1. Focus
2. Models
3. Systems
4. Breakthroughs

their current ceiling, and staying the forever apprentice. It's what writer and memory champion Joshua Foer dubbed the "OK Plateau." He illustrated it with typing. If practice time were all that mattered, over the course of our professional careers, with the millions of memos and e-mails we type, we'd all progress from the lowly chicken peck to 100 words a minute. But that doesn't happen. We reach a level of skill we deem to be acceptable and then simply switch off the learning. We go on automatic pilot and hit one of the most common ceilings of achievement: we hit the OK Plateau.

When you're in search of extraordinary results, accepting an OK Plateau or any other ceiling of achievement isn't okay when it applies to your ONE Thing. When you want to break through plateaus and ceilings, there is only one approach—"P."

In business and in life, we all start off entrepreneurially. We go after something with our current level of abilities, energy, knowledge, and effort—in short, everything that comes easily. Approaching things with "E" is comfortable because it feels natural. It's who we currently are and how we currently like to do things.

It's also limiting.

When "E" is our only approach, we create artificial limits to what we can achieve and who we can become. If we tackle something with all "E" and then hit a ceiling of achievement, we simply bounce up against it, over and over and over. This continues until we just can't take the disappointment anymore, become resigned to this being the only outcome we can ever have, and eventually seek out greener pastures elsewhere. When we think we've maxed out our potential in a situation, starting over is how we think we'll get ahead. The problem is this becomes a vicious cycle of taking on the next new thing with renewed enthusiasm, energy, natural ability, and effort, until another ceiling is hit and disappointment and resignation set in once again. And then it's on to—you guessed it—the next greener pasture.

Bring "P" to the same ceiling and things look different. The Purposeful approach says, "I'm still committed to growing, so what are my options?" You then use the Focusing Question to narrow those choices down to the next thing you should do. It could be to follow a new model, get a new system, or both. But be prepared. Implementing these may require new thinking, new skills, and even new relationships. Probably none of this will feel natural at first. That's okay. Being Purposeful is often about doing what comes "unnaturally," but when you're committed to achieving extraordinary results, you simply do whatever it takes anyway.

When you've done the best you can do but are certain the results aren't the best they can be, get out of "E" and into "P." Look for the better models and systems, the ways that can take you farther. Then adopt new thinking, new skills, and new relationships to help you put them into action. Become Purposeful during your time block, and unlock your potential.

3. LIVE THE ACCOUNTABILITY CYCLE

There is an undeniable connection between what you do and what you get. Actions determine outcomes, and outcomes inform actions. Be accountable and this feedback loop is how you discover the things you must do to achieve extraordinary results. That's why your final commitment is to live the accountability cycle of results.

Taking complete ownership of your outcomes by holding no one but yourself responsible for them is the most powerful thing you can do to drive your success. As such, accountability is most likely the most important of the three commitments. Without it, your journey down the path of mastery will be cut short the moment you encounter a challenge. Without it, you won't figure out how to break through the ceilings of achievement you'll hit along the way. Accountable people absorb setbacks and keep going. Accountable people persevere through problems and keep pushing forward. Accountable people are results oriented and never defend actions, skill levels, models, systems, or relationships that just aren't getting the job done. They bring their best to whatever it takes, without reservation.

Accountable people achieve results others only dream of.

When life happens, you can be either the author of your life or the victim of it. Those are your only two choices—accountable or unaccountable. This may sound harsh, but it's true. Every day we choose one approach or the other, and the consequences follow us forever.

To illustrate the difference, consider the tale of two managers of two competing businesses who both experience a sudden shift in the market. One month, there is a continuous line of customers stretching out the door. The next, no one shows up. How each manager responds makes all the difference.

The accountable manager immediately tunes in: *What's happening here?* She investigates exactly what she's up against. The other manager refuses to acknowledge what's happening. *It's a blip, a glitch, an anomaly.* He shrugs it off as simply a "bad month." Meanwhile, the accountable manager, having

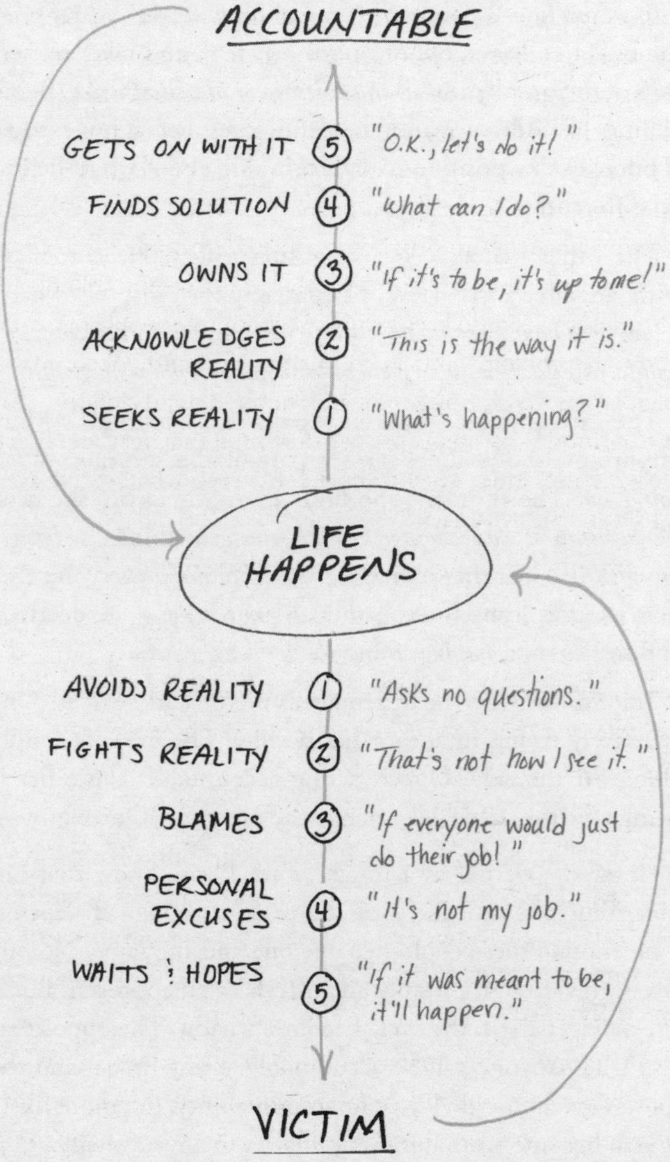

ACCOUNTABLE

GETS ON WITH IT	⑤	"O.K., let's do it!"
FINDS SOLUTION	④	"What can I do?"
OWNS IT	③	"If it's to be, it's up to me!"
ACKNOWLEDGES REALITY	②	"This is the way it is."
SEEKS REALITY	①	"What's happening?"

LIFE HAPPENS

AVOIDS REALITY	①	"Asks no questions."
FIGHTS REALITY	②	"That's not how I see it."
BLAMES	③	"If everyone would just do their job!"
PERSONAL EXCUSES	④	"It's not my job."
WAITS & HOPES	⑤	"If it was meant to be, it'll happen."

VICTIM

FIG. 32 Don't be a victim—live the cycle of accountability!

discovered how a competitor is grabbing market share, bites the bullet and says, *So, this is the way it is,* and takes ownership of the problem. *If it's to be, it's up to me,* she thinks. Being willing to address reality head-on gives her a huge edge. It puts her in a position to start thinking about what she can do differently.

The other manager keeps fighting reality. He comes up with an alternative view, placing responsibility elsewhere. *That's not how I see it,* he counters. *If people in the company would just do their jobs, we wouldn't have problems like this!*

The accountable manager looks for solutions. More important, she assumes she's a part of the solution: *What can I do?* The moment she finds the right tactic, she acts. *Circumstances won't change by themselves,* she thinks, so *let's get on with it!* The other manager, having blamed everyone else, now excuses himself altogether. *It's not my job,* he declares, and settles in to *hoping things change for the better.*

Told in this way, the difference is pretty stark, isn't it? One is actively trying to author her destiny. The other is simply along for the ride. One is acting accountable; the other is being a victim. One will change the outcome. One won't.

Granted, "victim" is a tough word. Please know that I'm describing the attitude, not the person, though if kept up long enough these could become one and the same. No one is a born victim; it's simply an attitude or an approach. But if allowed to persist, the cycle becomes a habit. The opposite is also true. Anyone can be accountable at any time—and the more you choose the cycle of accountability, the more likely it is to become your automatic answer to any adversity.

Highly successful people are clear about their role in the events of their life. They don't fear reality. They seek it, acknowledge it, and own it. They know this is the only way to uncover new solutions, apply them, and experience a different reality, so they take responsibility and run with it. They see outcomes as information they can use to frame better actions to get better outcomes. It's a cycle they understand and use to achieve extraordinary results.

One of the fastest ways to bring accountability to your life is to find an accountability partner. Accountability can come from a mentor, a peer or, in its highest form, a coach. Whatever the case, it's critical that you acquire an accountability relationship and give your partner license to lay out the honest truth. An accountability partner isn't a cheerleader, although he can lift you up. An accountability partner provides frank, objective feedback on your performance, creates an ongoing expectation for productive progress, and can provide critical brainstorming or even expertise when needed. As for me, a coach or a mentor is the best choice for an accountability partner. Although a peer or a friend can absolutely help you see things you may not see, ongoing accountability is best provided by someone to whom you agree to be truly accountable. When that's the nature of the relationship, the best results occur.

Earlier, I discussed Dr. Gail Matthews's research that individuals with written goals were 39.5 percent more likely to succeed. But there's more to the story. Individuals who wrote their goals and sent progress reports to friends were 76.7 percent more likely to achieve them. As effective as writing down your goals can be, simply sharing your progress toward your goals with someone regularly, even just a friend, makes you almost twice as effective.

Accountability works.

Ericsson's research on expert performance confirms the same relationship between elite performance and coaching. He observed that "the single most important difference between these amateurs and the three groups of elite performers is that the future elite performers seek out teachers and coaches and engage in supervised training, whereas the amateurs rarely engage in similar types of practice."

An accountability partner will positively impact your productivity. They'll keep you honest and on track. Just knowing they are waiting for your next progress report can spur you to better results. Ideally, a coach can "coach" you on how to maximize your performance over time. This is how the very best become the very best.

Coaching will help you with all three commitments to your ONE Thing. On the path to mastery, on the journey from "E" to "P," and in living the accountability cycle, a coach is invaluable. In fact, you'd be hard-pressed to find elite achievers who don't have coaches helping them in key areas of their life.

It's never too soon or too late to get a coach. Commit to achieving extraordinary results and you'll find a coach gives you the best chance possible.

BIG IDEAS

1. **Commit to be your best.** Extraordinary results happen only when you give the best you have to become the best you can be at your most important work. This is,

in essence, the path to mastery—and because mastery takes time, it takes a commitment to achieve it.

2. **Be purposeful about your ONE Thing.** Move from "E" to "P." Go on a quest for the models and systems that can take you the farthest. Don't just settle for what comes naturally—be open to new thinking, new skills, and new relationships. If the path of mastery is a commitment to be your best, being purposeful is a commitment to adopt the best possible approach.

3. **Take ownership of your outcomes.** If extraordinary results are what you want, being a victim won't work. Change occurs only when you're accountable. So stay out of the passenger seat and always choose the driver's side.

4. **Find a coach.** You'll be hard-pressed to find anyone who achieves extraordinary results without one.

Remember, we're not talking about ordinary results—extraordinary is what we're after. That kind of productivity eludes most, but it doesn't have to. When you time block your most important priority, protect your time block, and then work your time block as effectively as possible, you'll be as productive as you can be. You'll be living the power of The ONE Thing.

Now you just have to avoid getting hijacked.

17 THE FOUR THIEVES

> "Focus is a matter of deciding what things you're not going to do."
>
> —John Carmack

In 1973, a group of seminary students unknowingly participated in a grand study known as "The Good Samaritan Experiment." These students were recruited and divided into two groups to see what factors influenced whether or not they would help a stranger in distress. Some were told they were going to prepare a talk about seminary jobs; the others, that they were going to give a talk about the Parable of the Good Samaritan, a Biblical story about helping people in need. Within each group, some were told they were late and had to hurry to their destination, while others were told they could take their time. What the students didn't know was that researchers had planted a man along the way—slumped on the ground, coughing, apparently in distress.

In the end, fewer than half the students stopped to help. But the deciding factor wasn't the task—it was time. Ninety percent of the students who were rushed failed to stop and render aid to the stranger. Some actually stepped over him in their hurry to get where they were supposed to go. It didn't seem to matter that half of them were on their way to deliver a talk on helping others!

Now, if seminary students can so easily lose focus on their real priority, do the rest of us even have a prayer?

Clearly, our best intentions can easily be undone. Just as there are the Six Lies that will deceive and mislead you, there are Four Thieves that can hold you up and rob you of your productivity. And since there's no one standing by to protect you, it's up to you to stop these thieves in their tracks.

THE FOUR THIEVES OF PRODUCTIVITY

1. Inability to Say "No"
2. Fear of Chaos
3. Poor Health Habits
4. Environment Doesn't Support Your Goals

1. INABILITY TO SAY "NO"

Someone once told me that one "yes" must be defended over time by 1,000 "nos." Early in my career I didn't understand this at all. Today, I think it's an understatement.

It's one thing to be distracted when you're trying to focus, it's another entirely to be hijacked before you even get to. The way to protect what you've said yes to and stay productive is to say no to anyone or anything that could derail you.

Peers will ask for your advice and help. Co-workers will want you on their team. Friends will request your assistance. Strangers will seek you out. Invitations and interruptions will come at you from everywhere imaginable. How you handle all of this determines the time you're able to devote to your ONE Thing and the results you're ultimately able to produce.

Here's the thing. When you say yes to something, it's imperative that you understand what you're saying no to. Screenwriter Sidney Howard, of *Gone with the Wind* fame, advised, "One-half of knowing what you want is knowing what you must give up before you get it." In the end, the best way to succeed big is to go small. And when you go small, you say no—a lot. A lot more than you might have ever considered before.

No one knew how to go small better than Steve Jobs. He was famously as proud of the products he didn't pursue as he was of the transformative products Apple created. In the two years after his return in 1997, he took the company from 350 products to ten. That's 340 nos, not counting anything else proposed during that period. At the 1997 MacWorld Developers Conference, he explained, "When you think about focusing, you think, 'Well, focusing is saying yes.' No! Focusing is about saying no." Jobs was after extraordinary results and he knew there was only one way to get there. Jobs was a "no" man.

The art of saying yes is, by default, the art of saying no. Saying yes to everyone is the same as saying yes to nothing.

Each additional obligation chips away at your effectiveness at everything you try. So the more things you do, the less successful you are at any one of them. You can't please everyone, so don't try. In fact, when you try, the one person you absolutely won't please is yourself.

Remember, saying yes to your ONE Thing is your top priority. As long as you can keep this in perspective, saying no to anything that keeps you from keeping your time block should become something you can accept.

Then it's just a matter of how.

All of us struggle to some degree with saying no. There are many reasons. We want to be helpful. We don't want to be hurtful. We want to be caring and considerate. We don't want to seem callous and cold. All of this is totally understandable. Being needed is incredibly satisfying, and helping others can be deeply fulfilling. Focusing on our own goals to the exclusion of others, especially the causes and the people we value the most, can feel downright selfish and self-centered. But it doesn't have to.

Master marketer Seth Godin says, "You can say no with respect, you can say no promptly, and you can say no with a lead to someone who might say yes. But just saying yes because you can't bear the short-term pain of saying no is not going to help you do the work." Godin gets it. You can keep your yes and say no in a way that works for you and for others.

Of course, whenever you need to say no, you can just say it and be done with it. There is nothing wrong with this at all. In fact, this should be your first choice every time. But if you feel there are times you need to say no in a helpful way, there are many ways to say it that can still lead people forward toward their goals.

You can ask them a question that leads them to find the help they need elsewhere. You might suggest another approach that doesn't require any help at all. You might not know what else they could do, so you could help them by gently prompting them to get creative. You can politely redirect their request to others who might be better able to assist them.

Now, if you do end up saying yes, there are a variety of creative ways you can deliver it. In other words, you can leverage your yeses. Help desks, support centers, and information resources couldn't exist without this kind of strategic thinking. Preprinted scripts, frequently asked question pages or files, written explanations, recorded instructions, posted information, checklists, catalogs, directories, and prescheduled training classes can all be used to effectively say yes while still preserving your time block. I started doing this in my first job as sales manager. I leveraged training sessions to cut frequently asked questions off at the pass, and then by either printing or recording them, created a library of answers my team could access whenever I wasn't personally available.

The biggest lesson I've learned is that it helps to have a philosophy and an approach to managing my space. Over time I developed what I refer to as the "Three-Foot Rule." When I hold one of my arms out as widely as possible, from my neck to my fingertips is three feet. I've made it my time-managing mission to limit who and what can get within three feet of me. The rule is simple: A request must be connected to my ONE Thing for me to consider it. If it's not, then I either say no to it or use any one of the approaches I shared above to deflect it elsewhere.

Learning to say no isn't a recipe for being a recluse. Just the opposite. It's a way to gain the greatest freedom and flexibility possible. Your talent and abilities are limited resources. Your time is finite. If you don't make your life about what you say yes to, then it will almost certainly become what you intended to say no to.

In a 1977 article in *Ebony* magazine, the incredibly successful comedian Bill Cosby summed up this productivity thief perfectly. As he was building his career, Cosby read some advice that he took to heart: "I don't know the key to success, but the key to failure is trying to please everybody." This is advice worth living by. If you can't say no a lot, you'll never truly be able to say yes to achieving your ONE Thing. Literally, it's one or the other—and you get to decide.

When you give your ONE Thing your most emphatic "Yes!" and vigorously say "No!" to the rest, extraordinary results become possible.

2. FEAR OF CHAOS

A not-so-funny thing happens along the way to extraordinary results. Untidiness. Unrest. Disarray. Disorder. When we tirelessly work our time block, clutter automatically takes up residence around us.

Messes are inevitable when you focus on just one thing. While you whittle away on your most important work, the world doesn't sit and wait. It stays on fast forward and things just rack up and stack up while you bear down on a singular priority. Unfortunately, there's no pause or stop button. You can't run life in slow motion. Wishing you could will just make you miserable and disappointed.

One of the greatest thieves of productivity is the unwillingness to allow for chaos or the lack of creativity in dealing with it.

Focusing on ONE Thing has a guaranteed consequence: other things don't get done. Although that's exactly the point, it doesn't automatically make us feel any better about it. There will always be people and projects that simply aren't a part of your biggest single priority but still matter. You will feel them pressing for your attention. There will always be unfinished work and loose ends lying around to snare your focus. Your time block can feel like a submersible, where the deeper you commit to your ONE Thing, the more the pressure mounts for you to come up for air and address everything you've put on hold. Eventually it can feel like even the tiniest leak might trigger an all-out implosion.

When this happens, when you give in to the pressure of any chaos being left unattended, it can be a total relief. But not when it comes to productivity.

It's a thief!

The truth is, it's a package deal. When you strive for greatness, chaos is guaranteed to show up. In fact, other areas of your life may experience chaos in direct proportion to the time you put in on your ONE Thing. It's important for you to accept this instead of fighting it. Oscar-winning filmmaker Francis Ford Coppola warns us that "anything you build on a large scale or with intense passion invites chaos." In other words, get used to it and get over it.

Now, in anybody's life or work there are some things that just can't be ignored: family, friends, pets, personal commitments, or critical job projects. At any given time, you may have some or all of these tugging at your time block. You can't forgo your power hours, that's a given. So, what do you do?

> "If a cluttered desk is a sign of a cluttered mind, of what, then, is an empty desk a sign?"
>
> —Albert Einstein

I get asked this a lot. I'll be teaching and know that, as soon as I finish, hands are going to shoot up. "What do I do if I'm a single parent with kids?" "What if I have elderly parents who constantly depend on me?" "I have absolute obligations I must take care of, so what do I do?" These are obviously fair questions. Here's what I tell them.

Depending on your situation, your time block might initially look different from others'. Each of our situations is unique. Depending on where you are in your life, you may not be able to immediately block off every morning to be by yourself. You may have a kid or a parent in tow. You may be doing your time block at a day care, nursing home, or some other place you have to be. Your alone time may have to be at a different time of day for a while. You may have to trade off time with others so they protect your time block and you in turn protect theirs. You may even have your kids or parents help you during your time block because they simply must be with you or you actually need the support.

If you have to beg, then beg. If you have to barter, then barter. If you have to be creative, then be creative. Just don't be a victim of your circumstances. Don't sacrifice your time block on the altar of "I just can't make it work." My mom used to say, "When you argue for your limitations, you get to keep them," but this is one you can't afford. Figure it out. Find a way. Make it happen.

When you commit to your ONE Thing each day, extraordinary results ultimately occur. In time, this creates the income or opportunity to manage the chaos. So, don't let this thief pickpocket your productivity. Move past your fear of chaos, learn to deal with it, and trust that your work on your ONE Thing will come through for you.

3. POOR HEALTH HABITS

I was once asked, "If you don't take care of your body, where will you live?" It was a real question. I had been fighting the painful side effects of interstitial cystitis (you don't want to know) and was dealing with continually shaking legs, a debilitating side effect of cholesterol-fighting statins. My ability to function, much less focus, was extremely compromised, and the challenge to overcome this was daunting. My doctor gave me some options and asked me what I wanted to do. The answer was to change my health habits. It was then that I discovered one of the greatest lessons of extraordinary results:

Personal energy mismanagement is a silent thief of productivity.

When we keep borrowing against our future by poorly protecting our energy, there is a predictable outcome of either slowly running out of gas or prematurely crashing and burning. You see it all the time. When people don't understand the power of the ONE Thing, they try to do too much—and because this never works over time, they end up making a horrific deal with themselves. They go for success by sacrificing their health. They stay up late, miss meals or eat poorly, and completely ignore exercise. Personal energy becomes an afterthought; allowing health and home life to suffer becomes acceptable by default. Driven to hit goals, they think of cheating themselves as a good bet, but this gamble can't pay off. Not only does this approach consistently short-circuit your best work, it's dangerous to assume that health and hearth will be just waiting for you to come back and enjoy anytime in the future.

High achievement and extraordinary results require big energy. The trick is learning how to get it and keep it.

So, what can you do? Think of yourself as the amazing biological machine you are and consider this daily energy plan for high productivity. Begin early with meditation and prayer for spiritual energy; starting the day by connecting with your higher purpose aligns your thoughts and actions with a larger story. Then move straight to the kitchen for your most important meal of the day and the cornerstone of physical energy: a nutritious breakfast designed to fuel your day's work. You can't run long on empty calories, and you can't run at all on an empty tank. Figure out easy ways to eat right and then plan all your daily meals a week at a time.

Fueled up, head to your exercise spot to relieve stress and strengthen your body. Conditioning gives you maximum capacity, which is critical for maximum productivity. If you have limited time to exercise, the simple thing to do is to wear a pedometer. Toward the end of the day, if you haven't walked at least 10,000 steps, make it your ONE "exercise" Thing to reach your 10,000-step goal before you go to bed. This one habit will change your life.

Now, if you haven't spent time with your loved ones at breakfast or during your workout, go find them. Hug, talk, and laugh. You'll be reminded why you're working in the first place, and motivated to be as productive as possible so you can get home earlier. Productive people thrive on emotional energy; it fills their heart with joy and makes them light on their feet.

Next, grab your calendar and plan your day. Make sure you know what matters most, and make sure those things are going to get done. Look at what you have to do, estimate the time it will take to do them, and plan your time accordingly. Knowing what you must do and making the time to do it is how you bring the most amazing mental energy to your life. Calendaring your day this way frees your mind from worrying about what might not get done while inspiring you with what will. It's only when you make time for extraordinary results that they get a chance to show up.

When you get to work, go to work on your ONE Thing. If you're like me and have some morning priorities you must get done first, then give yourself an hour at most to do them. Don't loiter and don't slow down. Clear the decks and then get down to the business of doing what matters most. Around noon, take a break, have lunch, and turn your attention to everything else you can do before you head out for the day.

Last, in the evening when it's time for bed, get eight hours of sleep. Powerful engines need cooling down and resting before taking off again, and you're no different. You need your sleep so your mind and body can rest and recharge for tomorrow's extraordinary productivity. Anyone you know who gets little sleep and appears to be doing great is either a freak of nature or hiding its effects from you. Either way, they aren't your role model. Protect your sleep by determining when you must go to bed each night and don't allow yourself to be lured away from it. If you're committed to your wake-up time, you can stay up late only so many nights before you're forced to hit the hay at a decent hour. If your response is that you have too much to do, stop right now, go back to the beginning of this book, and start over. You apparently missed something. When you've connected proper sleep with success, you'll have a good enough reason to get up and you'll go to sleep at the right time.

THE HIGHLY PRODUCTIVE PERSON'S DAILY ENERGY PLAN

1. Meditate and pray for spiritual energy.
2. Eat right, exercise, and sleep sufficiently for physical energy.
3. Hug, kiss, and laugh with loved ones for emotional energy.
4. Set goals, plan, and calendar for mental energy.
5. Time block your ONE Thing for business energy.

Here's the productivity secret of this plan: when you spend the early hours energizing yourself, you get pulled through the rest of the day with little additional effort. You're not focused on having a perfect day all day, but on having an energized start to each day. If you can have a highly productive day until noon, the rest of the day falls easily into place. That's positive energy creating positive momentum. Structuring the early hours of each day is the simplest way to extraordinary results.

4. ENVIRONMENT DOESN'T SUPPORT YOUR GOALS

Early in my career, a married mom of two teenagers sat in front of me and cried. Her family had told her they would support her new career as long as nothing at home changed. Meals, carpooling, anything that touched their world couldn't be disrupted. She had agreed, only to discover later how bad a deal she'd cut. As I listened, I suddenly realized I was hearing about a productivity thief almost everyone overlooks.

Your environment must support your goals.

Your environment is simply who you see and what you experience every day. The people are familiar, the places comfortable. You trust these elements of your environment and quite possibly even take them for granted. But be aware. Anyone and anything at any time can become a thief, diverting your attention away from your most important work and stealing your productivity right from under your nose. For you to achieve extraordinary results, the people surrounding you and your physical surroundings must support your goals.

No one lives or works in isolation. Every day, throughout your day, you come in contact with others and are influenced by them. Unquestionably, these individuals impact your attitude, your health—and ultimately, your performance.

The people around you may be more important than you think. It's a fact that you're likely to pick up some of the attitudes of others by working with them, socializing with them, or simply being around them. From co-workers to friends to family, if they're generally not positive or fulfilled on the job or away from it, they'll probably pass on some of their negativity. Attitude is contagious; it spreads easily. As strong as you think you are, no one is strong enough to avoid the

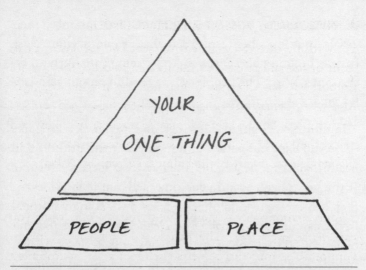

FIG. 33 Create a productivity-specific environment to support your ONE Thing.

influence of negativity forever. So, surrounding yourself with the right people is the right thing to do. While attitude thieves will rob you of energy, effort, and resolve, supportive people will do what they can to encourage or assist you. Ultimately, being with success-minded people creates what researchers call a "positive spiral of success" where they lift you up and send you on your way.

Who you hang out with also has serious implications for your health habits. Harvard professor Dr. Nicholas A. Christakis and University of California, San Diego associate professor James H. Fowler wrote the book on how our social networks unmistakably impact our well-being. Their book, *Connected: The Surprising Power of Our Social Networks and How They Shape Our Lives,* connects the dots between our relationships and drug use, sleeplessness, smoking, drinking, eating, and even happiness. For instance, their 2007 study on obesity revealed that if one of your close friends becomes obese, you're 57 percent more likely to do the same. Why? The people we see tend to set our standard for what's appropriate.

In time, you begin to think, act, and even look a little like those you hang out with. But not only do their attitudes and health habits influence you, their relative success does too. If the people you spend your time with are high achievers, their achievements can influence your own. A study featured in the psychology journal *Social Development* shows that out of nearly 500 school-age participants with reciprocal "best friend" relationships, "children who establish and maintain relationships with high-achieving students experience gains in their report card grades." Further, those who have high-achieving friends appear "to benefit with regard to their motivational beliefs and academic performance." Hanging out with people who seek success will strengthen your motivation and positively push your performance.

Your mother was right when she cautioned you to be careful of the company you keep. The wrong people in your environment can most certainly dissuade, deter, and distract you from the productivity course you've set out on. But the opposite is also true. No one succeeds alone and no one fails alone. Pay attention to the people around you. Seek out those who will support your goals, and show the door to anyone who won't. The individuals in your life will influence you and impact you—probably more than you give them credit for. Give them their due and make sure that the sway they have on you sends you in the direction you want to go.

If people are the first priority in creating a supportive environment, place isn't far behind. When your physical environment isn't in step with your goals, it can also keep you from ever getting started on them in the first place.

> "Surround yourself only with people who are going to lift you higher."
>
> —Oprah Winfrey

I know this sounds oversimplified, but to succeed at doing your ONE Thing you have to be able to get to it, and your physical environment plays a vital role in whether you do or not. The wrong surroundings may never let you get there. If your environment is so full of distractions and diversions that before you can help yourself you've gotten caught doing something you shouldn't, you won't get where you need to go. Think of it as having to walk down an aisle of candy every day when you're trying to lose weight. Some may be able to handle this easily, but most of us are going to sample some sweets along the way.

What is around you will either aim you toward your time block or pull you away. This starts from the time you wake up and continues until you get to your time-block bunker. What you see and hear from the time your alarm rings to when your time block begins ultimately determines if you get there, when you get there, and whether you're ready to be productive when you do. So, do a trial run. Walk through the path you'll take each day, and eradicate all the sight and sound thieves that you find. For me, at home it's simple things like e-mail, the morning paper, the morning TV news shows, the neighbors out walking their dogs. All wonderful things, but not wonderful when I have an appointment with myself to accomplish my ONE Thing. So, I check off e-mail quickly, I never see the paper, I keep the TV cabinet closed, and I choose my driving route carefully. At work, I avoid the community coffee pot and the information boards. They can come later in the day. What I've learned is that when you clear the path to success—that's when you consistently get there.

Don't let your environment lead you astray. Your physical surroundings matter and the people around you matter. Having an environment that doesn't support your goals is all too common, and unfortunately an all-too-common thief of productivity. As actor and comedian Lily Tomlin once said, "The road to success is always under construction." So don't allow yourself to be detoured from getting to your ONE Thing. Pave your way with the right people and place.

BIG IDEAS

1. **Start saying "no."** Always remember that when you say yes to something, you're saying no to everything else. It's the essence of keeping a commitment. Start turning down other requests outright or saying, "No, for now" to distractions so that nothing detracts you from getting to your top priority. Learning to say no can and will liberate you. It's how you'll find the time for your ONE Thing.

2. **Accept chaos.** Recognize that pursuing your ONE Thing moves other things to the back burner. Loose ends can feel like snares, creating tangles in your path. This kind of chaos is unavoidable. Make peace with it. Learn to deal with it. The success you have accomplishing your ONE Thing will continually prove you made the right decision.

3. **Manage your energy.** Don't sacrifice your health by trying to take on too much. Your body is an amazing machine, but it doesn't come with a warranty, you can't trade it in, and repairs can be costly. It's important to manage your energy so you can do what you must do, achieve what you want to achieve, and live the life you want to live.

4. **Take ownership of your environment.** Make sure that the people around you and your physical surroundings support your goals. The right people in your life and the right physical environment on your daily path will support your efforts to get to your ONE Thing. When both are in alignment with your ONE Thing, they will supply the optimism and physical lift you need to make your ONE Thing happen.

Screenwriter Leo Rosten pulled everything together for us when he said, "I cannot believe that the purpose of life is to be happy. I think the purpose of life is to be useful, to be responsible, to be compassionate. It is, above all, to matter, to count, to stand for something, to have made some difference that you lived at all." Live with Purpose, Live by Priority, and Live for Productivity. Follow these three for the same reason you make the three commitments and avoid the four thieves—because you want to leave your mark. You want your life to matter.

18 THE JOURNEY

"One step at a time" may be trite, but it's still true. No matter the objective, no matter the destination, the journey to anything you want always starts with a single step.

That step is called the ONE Thing.

I want you to do something. I want you to close your eyes and imagine your life as big as it can possibly be. As big as you have ever dared to dream, and then some. Can you see it?

Now, open your eyes and listen to me. Whatever you can see, you have the capacity to move toward. And when what you go for is as vast as you can possibly envision, you'll be living the biggest life you can possibly live.

Living large is that simple.

Let me share a way you can do this. Write down your current income. Then multiply it by a number: 2, 4, 10, 20—it doesn't matter. Just pick one, multiply your income by it, and write down the new number. Looking at it and ignoring whether you're frightened or excited, ask yourself, "Will my current actions get me to this number in the next five years?" If they will, then keep doubling the number until they won't. If you then make your actions match your answer, you'll be living large.

Now, I use personal earnings only as an example. This thinking can apply to your spiritual life, your physical conditioning, your personal relationships, your career achievement, your business success, or anything else that matters to you. When you lift the limits of your thinking, you expand the limits of your life. It's only when you can imagine a bigger life that you can ever hope to have one.

The challenge is that living the largest life possible requires you not only to think big, but also to take the necessary actions to get there.

Extraordinary results require you to go small.

Getting your focus as small as possible simplifies your thinking and crystallizes what you must do. No matter how big you can think, when you know where you're going and work backwards to what you need to do to get there, you'll always discover it begins with going small. Years ago, I wanted an apple tree on our property. Turns out you can't buy a fully mature one. The only option I had was to buy a small one and grow it. I could think big, but I had no choice but to start small. So I did, and five years later we had apples. But because I thought as big as I could, guess what? You got it. I didn't just plant one. Today—we have an orchard.

Your life is like this. You don't get a fully mature one. You get a small one and the opportunity to grow it—if you want to. Think small and your life's likely to stay small. Think big and your life has a chance to grow big. The choice is yours. When you choose a big life, by default, you'll have to go small to get there. You must survey your choices, narrow your options, line up your priorities, and do what matters most. You must go small. You must find your ONE Thing.

There is no surefire thing, but there's always something, ONE Thing, that out of everything matters more than anything. I'm not saying there will only be one thing, or even the same thing, forever. I'm saying that at any moment in time there can be only ONE Thing, and when that ONE Thing is in line with your purpose and sits atop your priorities, it will be the most productive thing you can do to launch you toward the best you can be.

Actions build on action. Habits build on habit. Success builds on success. The right domino knocks down another and another and another. So whenever you want extraordinary results, look for the levered action that will start a domino run for you. Big lives ride the powerful wave of chain reactions and are built sequentially, which means when you're aiming for success you can't just skip to the end. Extraordinary doesn't work like that. The knowledge and momentum that build as you live the ONE Thing each day, each week, each month, and each year are what give you the ability to build an extraordinary life.

> "Only those who will risk going too far can possibly find out how far one can go."
>
> —T. S. Eliot

But this doesn't just happen. You have to make it happen.

One evening an elder Cherokee told his grandson about a battle that goes on inside all people. He said, "My son, the battle is between two wolves inside us. One is Fear. It carries anxiety, concern, uncertainty, hesitancy, indecision and inaction. The other is Faith. It brings calm, conviction, confidence, enthusiasm, decisiveness, excitement and action." The grandson thought about it for a moment and then meekly asked his grandfather: "Which wolf wins?" The old Cherokee replied, *"The one you feed."*

Your journey toward extraordinary results will be built above all else on faith. It's only when you have faith in your purpose and priorities that you'll seek out your ONE Thing. And once certain you know it, you'll have the personal power necessary to push you through any hesitancy to do it. Faith ultimately leads to action, and when we take action we avoid the very thing that could undermine or undo everything we've worked for—regret.

ADVICE FROM A FRIEND

As satisfying as succeeding is, as fulfilling as journeying feels, there is actually an even better reason to get up every day and take action on your ONE Thing. On your way to living a life worth living, doing your best to succeed at what matters most to you not only rewards you with success and happiness but with something even more precious.

No regrets.

> "Twenty years from now you will be more disappointed by the things that you didn't do than by the ones you did do. So throw off the bowlines. Sail away from the safe harbor. Catch the trade winds in your sails. Explore. Dream. Discover."
>
> —Mark Twain

If you could go back in time and talk to the 18-year-young you or leap forward and visit with the 80-year-old you, who would you want to take advice from? It's an interesting proposition. For me, it would be my older self. The view from the stern comes with the wisdom gathered from a longer and wider lens.

So what would an older, wiser you say? "Go live your life. Live it fully, without fear. Live with purpose, give it your all, and never give up." Effort is important, for without it you will never succeed at your highest level. Achievement is important, for without it you will never experience your true potential. Pursuing purpose is important, for unless you do, you may never find lasting happiness. Step out on faith that these things are true. Go live a life worth living where, in the end, you'll be able to say, "I'm glad I did," not "I wish I had."

Why do I think this? Because many years ago I began trying to understand what a life worth living would look like. I decided to go out and discover what this might be. It was a trip worth taking. I visited with people older than me, wiser than me, more successful than me. I researched, I read, I sought advice. From every credible source imaginable, I looked for clues and signs. Ultimately I stumbled on a simple point of view: A life worth living might be measured in many ways, but the one way that stands above all others is living a life of no regrets.

Life is too short to pile up woulda, coulda, shouldas.

What clinched this for me was when I asked myself who might be the people with the greatest clarity about life. I decided it was those who were nearing the end of theirs. If starting with the end in mind is a good idea, then there's no end further than the very end of life to look for clues about how to live. I wondered what people with nothing left to do but look back might tell me about how to move forward. Their collective voice was overwhelming, the answer clear: live your life to minimize the regrets you might have at the end.

What kind of regrets? For me, very few books cause tears, much less require a handkerchief, but Bronnie Ware's 2012 book *The Top Five Regrets of the Dying* did both. Ware spent many years caring for those facing their own mortality. When she questioned the dying about any regrets they had or anything they would do differently, Bronnie found that common themes surfaced again and again. In descending order, the five most common were these: *I wish that I'd let myself be happier*—too late they realized happiness is a choice; *I wish I'd stayed in touch with my friends*—too often they failed to give them the time and effort they deserved; *I wish I'd had the courage to express my feelings*—too frequently shut mouths and shuttered feelings weighed too heavy to handle; *I wish I hadn't worked so hard*—too much time spent making a living over building a life caused too much remorse.

As tough as these were, one stood out above them all. The most common regret was this: *I wish I'd had the courage to live a life true to myself, not the life others expected of me.* Half-filled dreams and unfulfilled hopes: this was the number-one regret expressed by the dying. As Ware put it, "Most people had not honored even a half of their dreams and had to die knowing that it was due to choices they had made, or not made."

Bronnie Ware's observations aren't hers alone. At the conclusion of their exhaustive research, Gilovich and Medvec in 1994 wrote, "When people look back on their lives, it is the things they have *not* done that generate the greatest regret. . . . People's actions may be troublesome initially; it is their inactions that plague them most with long-term feelings of regret."

Honoring our hopes and pursuing productive lives through faith in our purpose and priorities is the message from our elders. From the wisest position they'll ever have comes their clearest message.

No regrets.

So make sure every day you do what matters most. When you know what matters most, everything makes sense. When you don't know what matters most, anything makes sense. The best lives aren't led this way.

SUCCESS IS AN INSIDE JOB

So, how do you live a life of no regrets? The same way your journey to extraordinary results begins. With purpose, priority, and productivity; with the knowledge that regret must be avoided, and can be; with your ONE Thing at the top of your mind and the top of your schedule; with a single first step we can all take.

I believe the best way to share this is in a story.

One evening, a young boy hopped up on his father's lap and whispered, "Dad, we don't spend enough time together." The father, who dearly loved his son, knew in his heart this was true and replied, "You're right and I'm so sorry. But I promise I'll make it up to you. Since tomorrow is Saturday, why don't we spend the entire day together? Just you and me!" It was a plan, and the boy went to bed that night with a smile on his face, envisioning the day, excited about the adventurous possibilities with his Pops.

The next morning the father rose earlier than usual. He wanted to make sure he could still enjoy his ritual cup of coffee with the morning paper before his son awoke, wound up and ready to go. Lost in thought reading the business section, he was caught by surprise when suddenly his son pulled the newspaper down and enthusiastically shouted, "Dad, I'm up. Let's play!"

The father, although thrilled to see his son and eager to start the day together, found himself guiltily craving just a little more time to finish his morning routine. Quickly racking his brain, he hit upon a promising idea. He grabbed his son, gave him a huge hug, and announced that their first game would be to put a puzzle together, and when that was done, "we'll head outside to play for the rest of the day."

Earlier in his reading, he had seen a full-page ad with a picture of the world. He quickly found it, tore it into little pieces, and spread them out on the table. He found some tape for his son and said, "I want to see how fast you can put this puzzle together." The boy enthusiastically dove right in, while his father, confident that he had now bought some extra time, buried himself back in his paper.

Within minutes, the boy once again yanked down his father's newspaper and proudly announced, "Dad, I'm done!" The father was astonished. For what lay in front of him—whole, intact, and complete—was the picture of the world, back together as it was in the ad and not one piece out of place. In a voice mixed with parental pride and wonder, the father asked, "How on earth did you do that so fast?"

The young boy beamed. "It was easy, Dad! I couldn't do it at first and I started to give up, it was so hard. But then I dropped a piece on the floor, and because it's a glass-top table, when I looked up I saw that there was a picture of a man on the other side. That gave me an idea!

"When I put the man together, the world just fell into place."

I first heard this innocent narrative when I was a teenager and I've never been able to shake it. It became a tale I continually retell in my head, and ultimately a central theme in my life. What struck me isn't the apparent issue with life balance the father had, though I certainly got that. What grabbed me and stuck with me was the inspired solution of the son. He cracked a deeper code: a simple and more straightforward approach to life. A starting point for any challenge we face personally or professionally. The ONE Thing we must all understand if we are to achieve extraordinary results at our highest level possible. Undoubtedly. Unquestionably.

Success is an inside job.

Put yourself together, and your world falls into place. When you bring purpose to your life, know your priorities, and achieve high productivity on the priority that matters most every day, your life makes sense and the extraordinary becomes possible.

All success in life starts within you. You know what to do. You know how to do it. Your next step is simple.

You are the first domino.

PUTTING THE ONE THING TO WORK

So what now?

You've read the book. You get it. You're ready to experience extraordinary results in your life. So, what do you do? How do you tap into The ONE Thing in the most powerful way? Let's revisit the heart of the book and look at ways you can put The ONE Thing to work right now.

For brevity's sake, I'll shorten the Focusing Question, so be sure to add "... such that by doing it everything will be easier or unnecessary?" at the end of each question!

YOUR PERSONAL LIFE

Let the ONE Thing bring clarity to the key areas of your life. Here's a short sampling.

- What's the ONE Thing I can do this week to discover or affirm my life's purpose ...?

- What's the ONE Thing I can do in 90 days to get in the physical shape I want ...?

- What's the ONE Thing I can do today to strengthen my spiritual faith ...?

- What's the ONE Thing I can do to find time to practice the guitar 20 minutes a day ...? Knock five strokes off my golf game in 90 days ...? Learn to paint in six months ...?

YOUR FAMILY

Use the ONE Thing with your family for fun and rewarding experiences. Here are some options.

- What's the ONE Thing we can do this week to improve our marriage ...?

- What's the ONE Thing we can do every week to spend more quality family time together ...?

- What's the ONE Thing we can do tonight to support our kid's schoolwork ...?

- What's the ONE Thing we can do to make our next vacation the best ever ...? Our next Christmas the best ever ...? Thanksgiving the best ever ...?

Please know that these are simply examples. If they apply to you personally, then great. If not, then use them to prompt you to discover what areas you might explore that matter to you.

And don't forget time blocking. Time block with yourself to make sure the things that matter get done and the activities that matter get mastered. In some cases, you'll want to block time to find your answer and, other times you'll just need to block time to implement it.

Now, let's go to work and see how you might take the power of the ONE Thing with you.

YOUR JOB

Put the ONE Thing to work taking your professional life to the next level. Here's a few ways to get started.

- What's the ONE Thing I can do today to complete my current project ahead of schedule . . . ?
- What's the ONE Thing I can do this month to produce better work . . . ?
- What's the ONE Thing I can do before my next review to get the raise I want . . . ?
- What's the ONE Thing I can do everyday to finish my work and still get home on time . . . ?

YOUR WORK TEAM

Pull the ONE Thing into your work with others. Whether you're a manager, executive, or even a business owner, bring ONE Thing thinking into your everyday work situations to drive productivity upward. Here are some scenarios to consider.

- In any meeting ask, "What's the ONE Thing we can accomplish in this meeting and end early . . . ?
- In building your team ask, What's the ONE Thing I can do in the next six months to find and develop incredible talent . . . ?

- In planning for the next month, year, or five years ask, What's the ONE Thing we can do right now to accomplish our goals ahead of schedule and under budget ... ?

- In your department or at the highest company level ask, What's the ONE Thing we can do in the next 90 days to create a ONE Thing culture ... ?

Again, these are merely examples to get you thinking about the possibilities. And, just as in your personal life, once you've decided what matters most, professional time blocking becomes your way of making sure it gets done. At work, this is usually about either a short-term project you must complete or an ongoing long-term activity you're committed to doing repeatedly. No matter, an appointment with yourself is the surest path to ensuring you achieve extraordinary results.

Casual open discussions or short in-house workshops around key concepts in the book might really help everyone at work find their own understanding and get on the same page.

If implementing the ONE Thing in an area requires you to involve others, consider getting them their own copy of the book. Sharing your ahas is a great start and you may be happily surprised with the insights you get back when others have a chance to read the book on their own.

Keep in mind that it takes more than reading the book and a few conversations or mentions in a meeting to make The ONE Thing a new habit in your life or in the lives of those around you. You know from reading the book that it takes on average 66 days to create a new habit, so approach this accordingly. To ignite your life you must focus on ONE Thing long enough for it to catch fire.

Let's look at a few other areas where The ONE Thing might make a real difference.

YOUR NON-PROFIT

What's the ONE Thing we can do to fund our annual financial needs...? Serve twice as many people...? Double our number of volunteers...?

YOUR SCHOOL

What's the ONE Thing we can do to decrease our dropout rate to zero ...? Raise our test scores by 20 percent ...? Increase our graduation rate to 100 percent ...? Double our parent participation...?

YOUR PLACE OF WORSHIP

What's the ONE Thing we can do to improve our worship experience...? Double our mission outreach success...? Max out our attendance ...? Achieve our finance goals ...?

YOUR COMMUNITY

What's the ONE Thing we can do to improve our sense of community...? Help the homebound...? Double our volunteerism...? Double voter turnout...?

After my wife Mary read this book, I asked her to do something. She turned to me and you know what she said? "Gary, that's not my ONE Thing right now!" We laughed, high-fived, and I got to do it myself!

The ONE Thing forces you to think big, work things through to create a list, prioritize that list so that a geometric progression can happen, and then hammer away on the first thing—the ONE Thing that starts your domino run.

So be prepared to live a new life! And remember that the secret to extraordinary results is to ask a very big and specific question that leads you to one very small and tightly focused answer.

If you try to do everything, you could wind up with nothing. If you try to do just ONE Thing, the right ONE Thing, you could wind up with everything you ever wanted.

The ONE Thing is real. If you put it to work, it will work.

So don't delay. Ask yourself the question, "What's the ONE Thing I can do right now to start using The ONE Thing in my life such that by doing it everything else will be easier or unnecessary?"

And make doing the answer your first ONE Thing!

Onward . . .

ON THE RESEARCH

Although I've lived the lessons of this book for some time, we began researching The ONE Thing in earnest in 2008. Since then, we've archived a collection of well over a thousand scholarly articles, scientific studies, and academic papers; hundreds of newspaper and magazine articles; and a large library of books written by the foremost experts in their fields. Binder after binder of discoveries, facts, and anecdotes literally covered every inch of our writing space.

If you want to dive deeper into what you've learned from this book, you can find an extensive list of our references organized by topic and by chapter at **The1Thing.com**.

This website is a gateway into our minds—we mention the authors who have inspired us, provide links to articles that are available online, and list those white papers that educated our thinking. We've also thrown in some additional interesting factoids and even a fun video here and there. Enjoy the journey.

INDEX

ACKNOWLEDGMENTS

When we were putting this book together, we agreed to do our best to organize it using the principles of The ONE Thing. Most books follow the Chicago Manual of Style's traditional guidelines and have a half-title, title, copyright, endorsements, author bio, foreword, acknowledgments, dedication, and epigraph pages all before you ever get to the table of contents and the actual text. Really?

It all got tossed out the window. In terms of advocating for you, the reader, we felt this was the ONE "design" Thing we could do to improve your experience. As a result, the acknowledgments ended up in the back of the book. In reality, if you were to reorder the book in terms of what's most important to the authors, this section may well have fallen just inside the front cover.

We began outlining this book in the summer of 2008 and submitted the first full draft to our publisher on June 1, 2012—a four-year journey we certainly couldn't have navigated without help. Lots of it.

Family comes first. Without the love and support of my wife Mary and son John, this book wouldn't be what it is. My writing partner, Jay, is equally thankful for the love and encouragement from Wendy and his kids, Gus and Veronica. Spouses, especially wise, literate ones like ours, get the largely thankless job of reading all the rough drafts rife with flaws and riddled with errors that eventually become a finished book.

We also benefited from a great support team. Vickie Lukachik and Kylah Magee loaded us up with so much research it took us close to half a year to digest it. Valerie Vogler-Stipe and Sarah Zimmerman did their ONE Thing and kept our plates and calendars free so we could stay focused on the book. The rest of our team, Allison Odom, Barbara Sagnes, Mindy Hager, Liz Krakow, Lisa Weathers, Denice Neason, and Mitch Johnson, also stayed on their ONE Thing so we could do ours.

My Keller Williams Realty partners and senior leaders each lent their ideas and support along the way: Mo Anderson, Mark Willis, Mary Tennant, Chris Heller, John Davis, Tony Dicello, Dianna and Shon Kokoszka, and Jim Talbot. Thanks guys! You rock! Our marketing team, led by Ellen Marks, worked extensively on the design of the book, including all the ways you likely heard about it: Annie Switt, Hiliary Kolb, Stephanie Van Hoek, Laura Price, the super-talented designers Michael Balistreri and Caitlin McIntosh, as well as Tamara Hurwitz, Jeff Ryder, and Owen Gibbs on our production team, and the web team of Hunter Frazier and Veronica Diaz. Cary Sylvester, Mike Malinowski, and Ben Herndon coordinated our IT work inside and outside the building with partners like Feed Magnet and NVNTD. Anthony Azar, Tom Freireich, and Danny Thompson worked with our vendor partners as well as with our partners in the field to make sure we got the book in as many hands as possible. Special thanks to Kaitlin Merchant of KW Research and Mona Covey, Julie Fantechi, and Dawn Sroka of KWU for their work pre- and post-publication.

We also had the benefit of working with a publisher that truly gets The ONE Thing and lives it, Ray Bard of Bard Press. He assembled an excellent team that advised, supported, and encouraged us when we were writing and later, during the editing, pushed us to the edge to make it as good as it could be. Our extended publishing team includes managing editor Sherry Sprague, editor Jeff Morris, copy/production editor Deborah Costenbader, Randy Miyake and Gary Hespenheide of Hespenheide Design, proofreader Luke Torn, and indexer Linda Webster.

Publicist Barbara Henricks of Cave Henricks Communications and social media pro Rusty Shelton of Shelton Interactive provided early feedback and led the media campaign. We also had a group of veteran readers who, with some select members of our team, provided feedback on our early draft: Jennifer Driscoll-Hollis, Spencer Gale, David Hathaway, Robert M. Hooper, Ph.D., Scott Provence, Cynthia Robbins, Robert Todd, and Todd Sattersten.

Thanks to the super-responsive researchers, professors, and authors who answered our questions on a variety of topics: Dr. Roy Baumeister, a Francis Eppes Eminent Scholar at Florida State University and Social Psychology Area Director; Dr. Myron P. Gutmann, Directorate for the Social, Behavioral, and Economic Sciences at the National Science Foundation; Dr. Eric Klinger, Professor of Psychology Emeritus at the University of Minnesota, Morris; Dr. Jonathan Levav, Associate Professor of Marketing at Stanford University; Paul McFedries, author of the unique website wordspy.com; Dr. David E. Meyer, Professor of Psychology in the Cognition and Perception Program at the University of Michigan and director of the University of Michigan's Brain, Cognition, and Action Laboratory; Dr. Phyllis Moen, McKnight Presidential Chair in Sociology at the University of Minnesota; Erica Mosner at Historical Studies–Social Science Library at the Institute for Advanced Study; the super-helpful Rachel from Bronnie Ware's website; Valoise Armstrong at the Dwight D. Eisenhower Library; Dr. Ed Deiner, author and Professor Emeritus in the Department of Psychology at the University of Illinois; and James Cathcart, Senior Leadership Consultant at Franklin Covey. We're also grateful to The Keller Center in the Hankamer School of Business at Baylor University and Casey Blaine for her research on multitasking early on in our journey.

And last, I'd be remiss if I didn't thank my business coach Bayne Henyon for his insights all those years ago that changed the way I looked at things and reshaped the way I worked.

Thank you everyone for everything!

ABOUT THE AUTHORS

GARY KELLER

Professionally, Gary's ONE Thing is teaching. He excelled as a real estate salesperson by teaching clients how to make great home buying-and-selling decisions. As a real estate sales manager, he recruited agents through training and helped them build their careers the same way. As cofounder and chairman of the board, he built Keller Williams Realty International from a single office in Austin, Texas, to the #1 position as the largest real estate company in the United States by using his skills as a teacher, trainer, and coach. Gary defines leadership as "teaching people how to think the way they need to think

GARY

JAY

so they can do what they need to do when they need to do it, so they can get what they want when they want it."

An Ernst & Young Entrepreneur of the Year and finalist for *Inc.* magazine's Entrepreneur of the Year, Keller is recognized as one of the most influential leaders in the real estate industry. He has also helped many small business owners and entrepreneurs find success through three nationally bestselling books: *The Millionaire Real Estate Agent*, *The Millionaire Real Estate Investor*, and *SHIFT: How Top Real Estate Agents Tackle Tough Times*. A book, after all, is just another way to teach, but one with an infinitely large classroom. As a business coach and national trainer, Gary has helped countless others realize extraordinary results by narrowing their focus to their own ONE Thing.

Unsurprising to those who know him, Gary believes that his single greatest achievement is the life he's built with his wife Mary and their son John.

JAY PAPASAN

Jay is the executive editor and vice president of publishing at Keller Williams Realty and president of Rellek Publishing. Professionally, his ONE Thing is writing. He attempted to write his first book on an electric typewriter in junior high and was hooked. At least one high school teacher thought his writing had promise and circulated one of his essays to the entire staff. Jay paid the bills in college by working in a bookstore. He got his undergraduate degree in writing and later, his Master's. After graduation, Jay took a job in publishing. During his years at HarperCollins in New York he worked on bestselling titles like *Body for Life* by Bill Phillips and *Go for the Goal* by Mia Hamm. More recently, in the ten years he's worked with Gary, Jay has coauthored numerous award-winning or bestselling titles, including the Millionaire Real Estate series.

Jay is passionate about sharing the ideas in his books and regularly speaks at conventions and training events. He is a member of the Keller Williams University International Master Faculty.

Outside of work, Jay co-owns a successful real estate investment business and sales team with his wife Wendy. They enjoy life in Austin, Texas, with their children Gus and Veronica.

WHAT'S THE
ONE
THING
I CAN DO
RIGHT NOW?

Now that you understand the concept, it's time to put The ONE Thing into action in your life. Visit **The1Thing.com** to start thinking big by going small and focusing on your ONE Thing today! Find up-to-date information on our seminars and coaching programs, as well as exclusive ONE Thing tools. See real-time updates from others joining the world-wide movement and share your ONE Thing. Experience your ONE Thing today.

First published in Great Britain in 2013 by John Murray (Publishers)
An Hachette UK Company

First published in the US in 2013 by Bard Press.

This edition published 2014

1

A CIP catalogue record for this title is available from the British Library

ISBN 9781848549258
Ebook ISBN 9781848549234

Printed and bound by Clays Ltd, St Ives plc

John Murray policy is to use papers that are natural, renewable and
recyclable products and made from wood grown in sustainable forests. The
logging and manufacturing processes are expected to conform to the
environmental regulations of the country of origin.

John Murray (Publishers)
338 Euston Road
London NW1 3BH

www.johnmurray.co.uk